A Resident's Recollections

by Lloyd E. Klos

Empire State Books
Interlaken, New York 14847
1987

Copyright © 1987
Lloyd E. Klos
All rights reserved

Pictures on Covers

Front: Trolley in Seneca Park Loop; Doc Bebko at RKO Palace Wurlitzer console; Rochester-Cobourg Car Ferry

Back: U.S.S. *Akron* in flight; Lowell Thomas

Library of Congress Cataloging in Publication

Klos, Lloyd E., 1922-
A resident's recollections / by Lloyd E. Klos.
p. cm.
1. Rochester Region (N.Y.)—Social life and customs. 2. Rochester Region (N.Y.)—History, Local. 3. New York (State)—Social life and customs. 4. New York (State)—History, Local. I. Title.
F129.R75K58 1987 974.7'8904-dc19 87-18918
ISBN: 0-932334-58-X (pbk)

ISBN: 0-932334-58-X
Manufactured in the United States of America

A *quality* publication of
Heart of the Lakes Publishing
Interlaken, New York 14847

DEDICATION

To my Mother and Father, Teresa H. and James A. Klos, whose encouragement spurred me toward better utilization of my writing talent in the first place.

And to Lucy R. Goodyear, a very special and dear friend, who found me lying on the Log of Procrastination and pushed me off into the Waters of Action to finally produce this book.

L. E. K.

CONTENTS

FOREWORD

This book amply represents the breadth of Lloyd Klos' interests and his skills as a writer. Over a period of many years he has transformed his interests into investigations which have continually surprised and delighted his readers.

Although best known for his definitive research into and writings about street railways, his insatiable curiosity has led him into many other fields. He has a knack of turning up ideas and details which continually delight.

For many years a newspaper librarian, he shows in his work an astonishing ability at research. This first surfaced for a wider audience in his articles on street railways. These combined not only a complete grasp of the mechanical and engineering aspects of this remarkable means of transportation, but brought back with nostalgia the years when these railways played so useful and enjoyable a role in the lives of most Americans.

This current book shows other aspects of Klos' repertoire. We are sure it will delight a growing circle of readers.

Andrew D. Wolfe

INTRODUCTION

This is not a book in the ordinary sense. It does not tell a story, it is not a biography, and it does not relate in chronological succession a series of events which centered on an occurence in history. It is a compendium, a collection of some of my writings which have appeared in the newspapers of the Wolfe Publications, Inc. in the Rochester, New York area.

From the time in May 1927 when father arrived home from work, saying, "There's a young fellow who's going to try to fly the Atlantic alone; they're calling him The 'Flying Fool'," the writer has been historically-minded. My best marks in school were attained in American History; the worst in tests following required readings of fiction.

Starting in May 1975, I combined this love of history, a reasonably good memory, and a modest talent for writing and came up with a monthly series of epics, entitled "A Resident's Recollections."

For this book, I've culled a variety of items, the majority centered in Upstate New York. A few have gone outside that area. And where typographical errors and changes in my original newspaper text occurred, I have corrected them. The date atop each article refers to the original publication date so that the reader will understand changes which may have occurred since, such as deaths. For any errors of fact, the writer assumes full responsibility.

I trust that the readers will like this, my initial book. Perhaps if it enjoys a modicum of success, a second will be forthcoming, encompassing greater scopes of area and material.

In the meantime, read, learn, but above all, enjoy.

Lloyd E. Klos
Irondequoit, New York
1987

PRETTY FAIR
COUNTRY ATHLETES

May 1975

In these times, people are prone to label persons, places and things "super." In the sports world, this monicker has become overused, whether it is applied to professional athletes or to those of high school calibre.

Back in the thirties at Irondequoit High School, we had some pretty fair country athletes whom we suspect could hold their own with the present crop. In those days, there were three sports at IHS, that's all: football, basketball, and baseball—a sport for each season.

The school term opened the day after Labor Day, but football practice started a couple weeks before. Besides Irondequoit (known as "The Baysiders" then), the county league included Webster, East Rochester, Fairport and the traditional rival, Brighton. Non-league games with Clyde, Perry, Caledonia or St. Francis DeSales of Geneva filled out the schedule.

When football's season ended in November, basketball took over with the first game, a non-league affair with Charlotte High on Thanksgiving Night. The league was expanded for this sport with the addition of Brockport and Spencerport in home-and-home series. The reserve team of sophomores and others who didn't make the varsity, was always featured in a preliminary game

Old Irondequoit High School which produced some fine athletes in its heyday. The front portion was built in 1895 with succeeding additions in 1908, 1922 and 1937.

with their counterpart.

When Spring came, baseball was the game, and the league included Irondequoit, Brighton, Hilton, Brockport, East Rochester and Spencerport.

The names of the athletes who sparked IHS teams in the thirties will be remembered not by being labeled "superstars," but by their participating in two or three sports and being named to all-county teams by the daily papers. Incidentally, interviews with athletes were not as frequent then. Their deeds meant more than their words.

Who can forget Bob Collett, Bob DeWeese, Harry Horn, Ken Jamieson, Bob Klippel, Raymond "Red" Moran, Ross Muxworthy, Dwight "Bud" Palmer, Bob Revard (all six-foot six of him), Phil Steinbacher and Don Whalen? There were others whose names escape us at the moment, but the above were remembered as those who indelibly left their names in IHS sports history.

Coaching the teams in the thirties was Royal W. Brown, a man with a gruff exterior, but one who personified the zenith in clean living. Not only did he coach high school athletics, but he also ran boys' physical ed (called "gym" then) in the upper grades at Hosea Rogers and Reuben Dake Schools, driving from place to place in a sleek, black Auburn roadster.

"Mr. Brown," as we respectfully addressed him, was always neatly attired with tie and white shirt. Besides his advice on the evils of tobacco and alcohol, Mr. Brown gave extensive instruction in close-order drill, and those of us who were to serve Uncle Sam a few years later owe him a debt of gratitude, as we didn't have to learn this phase of military discipline "cold" at the training camp. We recall the day at Hosea Rogers when Mr. Brown lined us up and gave the commands of preparation and execution. Anyone who performed wrongly was dropped from the line until two of us remained. When my classmate, Ray Elliott, made a mis-step, I was judged the winner.

Coach Brown's insistence that his athletes refrain from tobacco was a factor in his leaving Irondequoit, as I learned later. Any athlete, whether he be the star quarterback, center, or first baseman, and if caught smoking at Rothmund's Confectionary down the street, or anywhere else, was automatically suspended. This did not set well with doting parents who applied pressure on the District 3 School Board, and Brown's contract was not renewed after the 1936–37 school year. He eventually coached at Charlotte High.

So, the school board looked for someone with more liberal attitudes, and it certainly found him in Ken Anderson from Falconer, New York. This coach allowed his charges free reign. For example, in the Spring or Fall, he'd park his Ford sedan under the trees adjoining the Cooper Road athletic field, listen to its radio, and smoke while his charges indulged in any sport activity they chose.

He overlooked four-letter words which some uncouth students were prone to use at will. Anderson, though his football teams showed improvement over previous seasons, was dropped after three terms, and the respected Gordon Allen was installed. Bill Mammosser, a commercial studies teacher out of Syracuse University, coached football.

Sports at Irondequoit High have come a long way since the days of Royal W. Brown in the thirties. But, with all the awards given today, the adoration, the publicity and the overuse of the term "super," we wonder if the achievements of the high school athlete had more meaningful accomplishment then. It is something which could be the topic of discussion, well into the night.

MEETING THE GREAT AND NEAR GREAT

December 1975

It has been my good fortune to meet some of the great and near great. Following are my impressions of the noted with whom I have come in contact:

MEL ALLEN. We met the Voice of the Yankees after an extremely long double header, followed by his trip to Rochester, and he was not in a talkative mood when autographing his book in McCurdy's.

DR. EDWARD J. BEBKO. This musician-traveler and the Sage of Olean, N.Y., once worked on a New York radio series "Famous Fathers" which featured such noted personalities as Lauritz Melchoir, Lowell Thomas, Admiral Byrd, Jimmy Dorsey, Morton Downer, Ozzie Nelson, Clarence Chamberlain, Deems Taylor, Harry Langdon, Otis Skinner, Howard Lindsay, and Nick Kenney. The tales he has told us about them, have made Doc a favorite story-teller of ours.

THOMAS E. BRODERICK. The Irondequoit Supervisor from 1927 to 1949, and a power in local and state GOPolitics, was friendly, but not given to much humor. He always addressed us as "Sonny." "Serious" is the best word to describe him.

CARL CARMER. It is wise for a budding writer to ask a professional for advice. "Be accurate!" was Mr. Carmer's admonition; and this is what we've tried to be ever since we met him in Sibley's book department.

HENRY W. CLUNE. A gifted writer, he is perhaps the most modest man you'll find locally. Success hasn't gone to his head, and if a favor is done him, he is most profuse in his appreciation. A beautiful man!

HELEN DELL. The Los Angeles Dodger organist is one of the most happy persons we have known. Playing for her favorite baseball team helps! A fine musician, a meticulous programmer, a sparkling personality, and a delight to interview.

JOSEPH J. DURNHERR. The ace Times-Union cameraman picked us up one morning while waiting for a bus, enroute to work. Besides his proclivities with the camera, he had a love for people and a zest for living unmatched by most. Like the time he jumped into a pool at the Terrace Gardens to "rescue" actress Jean Harlow. The water was all of four inches deep! Once he announced his arrival at the "paragraph factory" by blowing a bugle, enroute to the darkroom.

FRANKIE FRISCH. The "Fordham Flash" was a veritable walking encyclopedia of baseball when we asked questions of him in Anchorage, Alaska in 1943.

FRANK E. GANNETT. We met publisher Gannett at the height of the Rochester newspaper strike in 1947, but he seemed unperturbed. What impressed us most was his neat, well-tailored appearance.

LILLIAN GISH. This diminutive actress, an authority on the silent movie era, exuded charisma when autographing her book after a lecture at East High School. One of the great artists of her profession.

BENNY GOODMAN. He is a big man, physically, and following an Eastman Theatre concert, placed his clarinet case under his arm, stuck his hands into his overcoat pockets, and nonchalantly walked up the street to the Sheraton. Benny has never forgotten his humble beginnings in Chicago.

RAY HYLAN. This local pioneer flyer has been closely associated with the growth of commercial and military aviation. Spending a couple hours with this "Early Bird," proved him to be an inexhaustible storehouse of aviation information, having known Eddie Rickenbacker, Jimmy Doolittle, Blanche Stuart Scott, Charles A. Lindbergh, Henry "Hap" Arnold, Carl "Tooey" Spaatz, Howard Hughes, Charles E. Rosendahl, Douglas Corrigan, Amelia Earhart, Russell Holderman and many others.

LEATRICE JOY. Every inch the distinguished actress, emphasized by her well-tailored gown; and by her half-block-long limousine which was awaiting her out front of Loew's 175th Street Theatre in New York in 1970.

JOHN ADAMS LOWE. A direct descendant of the famous Adams family of Massachusetts, this Rochester Public Library director was a kindly, friendly man who was intensely proud of the Rundel Memorial Building whose inscriptions on the facade he selected.

STAN MUSIAL. On a tour of Alaska in November, 1943, ex-Red Wing Stan easily mixed with the GIs while sitting on the floor of the Kashim Club at Fort Richardson near Anchorage, discussing baseball. An extremely modest, happy man who has not changed, even with Hall of Fame status.

JOSEPH J. O'BRIEN. This ex-Navy wrestler and East Rochester carshop foreman, became a congressman about 1939. A hail fellow, well-met, he always greeted those whose names easily eluded him, with the salutation, "Hello, Jack!"

ALEXANDER RUSSELL. The six-foot-six president of the old Rochester and Lake Ontario Water Service Corp. is never at a loss for words. A staunch Republican and lover of his country, he

Gloria Swanson in 1952. "We didn't need dialogue; we had faces," she said. And having one she knew how to use it!

once tutored President Theodore Roosevelt's children and was a tennis partner of TR. He now lives in Arizona.

JOHN A. SLATTERY. Just about the most popular fire chief in Rochester's history, Chief Slattery never exposed his men to danger to which he wouldn't expose himself, but it was automatic that whenever a multiple-alarm fire was raging, St. Mary's Hospital readied a room for him. A short, stocky, friendly man, he had a pair of hands which looked like hams and a grip like a vise.

GLORIA SWANSON. Though of small physical stature, ex-movie queen Gloria has only to step inside a door and she fills the room. During the two hours in her company in 1974, we found that she was capable of charm; but we suspect she can forcefully assert herself if the occasion demands. She once said of silent movies: "We didn't need dialogue; we had faces." And having one, she certainly uses it!

JUDY WEIS. Ever listen to a speaker whom you wished would have talked more? The irrepressible Judy, a power in "GOPolitics" was one of these; and it is a rare gift! Blessed with a winning personality, she had great executive and organizational ability.

ROGER WILLIAMS. When a youngster, this great popular pianist once stood in the rain to see Paderewski who didn't show. Roger vowed that if he became a concert artist, he'd meet his public. This gives a marvelous insight into the man who got his professional start (with Carl Dengler's help) in Leo DeLeo's Five O'Clock Club here. Extremely modest, gracious to all and a gentleman of the first order, egotist is one word which certainly doesn't describe him.

LOIS WILSON. This silent film star is still attractive and vivacious, and looks as if she could perform before the cameras today.

Prepare in Duplicate

(Local Board Date Stamp With Code)

Jan 11 1943
(Date of mailing)

ORDER TO REPORT FOR INDUCTION

The President of the United States,

To Lloyd (First name) Edward (Middle name) Klos (Last name)

Order No. 12 774

GREETING:

Having submitted yourself to a local board composed of your neighbors for the purpose of determining your availability for training and service in the armed forces of the United States, you are hereby

notified that you have now been selected for training and service in the Army (Army, Navy, Marine Corps)

You will, therefore, report to the local board named above at Abraham Lincoln School, off Norton Carl St. (Place of reporting)

at 7 (Hour of reporting) m., on the ______ day of Jan, 19 43

This local board will furnish transportation to an induction station of the service for which you have been selected. You will there be examined, and, if accepted for training and service, you will then be inducted into the stated branch of the service.

Persons reporting to the induction station in some instances may be rejected for physical or other reasons. It is well to keep this in mind in arranging your affairs, to prevent any undue hardship if you are rejected at the induction station. If you are employed, you should advise your employer of this notice and of the possibility that you may not be accepted at the induction station. Your employer can then be prepared to replace you if you are accepted, or to continue your employment if you are rejected.

Willful failure to report promptly to this local board at the hour and on the day named in this notice is a violation of the Selective Training and Service Act of 1940, as amended, and subjects the violator to fine and imprisonment. Bring with you sufficient clothing for 3 days.

You must keep this form and bring it with you when you report to the local board.

If you are so far removed from your own local board that reporting in compliance with this order will be a serious hardship and you desire to report to a local board in the area of which you are now located, go immediately to that local board and make written request for transfer of your delivery for induction, taking this order with you.

Member or clerk of the local board.

D. S. S. Form 150
(Revised 6-15-42)

U. S. GOVERNMENT PRINTING OFFICE 16—18271-2

Over ten million young men received these "Greetings from the President," the order to report for induction in World War II.

YOU'RE IN THE ARMY NOW!

January 1976

There rarely has been a January 21 or 28 since World War II when we haven't paused to remember what happened to us on those days in 1943. We're sure that many of the 150 young men in our special peer group of that time haven't forgotten what happened to them, either.

By the Summer of 1940, the Nazis had swept into Western Europe, and their war machine was poised at the English Channel for an expected invasion of Britain. In America, Congress debated the first peace-time military draft. Senator Edward Burke of Nebraska and Representative James W. Wadsworth of Geneseo, N.Y. were co-sponsors of a bill for conscription. Over vociferous protests of anti-war people, the measure eventually passed and draft boards were set up to handle registration to create a reservoir of manpower for the armed services.

Our Board was No. 558. The chairman was George B. McAvoy, a power in American Legion affairs. There was an advisory committee to aid prospective inductees, consisting of chairman Gerald R. Stoddart, C. Willard Burt, Frederick J. Mix, Charles Van Voorhis, Willard P. Curry, Frank E. Donnelly, Ford J. Decker and G. W. Austin Haines. As we recall, Board 558 had jurisdiction over draftees in Irondequoit and Rochester's 24th Ward.

Our first communique from the board was in June 1942,

directing us to appear at its offices in the old Irondequoit Town Hall on East Ridge Road. We filled out a registration card and were given a "registration certificate" card DSS Form 2 which stated: "The Law requires you to have this card in your personal possession at all times." It was signed by Otto Kupfer. No such things as draftcard burners then! One respected the laws.

Came early November 1942, the postman delivered a lengthy Selective Service questionnaire, giving us a month to fill it out. We wonder how many sent theirs in within a week! The questionnaire enabled Uncle Sam to obtain a chronology of one's life: education, employment, special talents, etc. "You will be classified on the basis of the information in your questionnaire," it stated, "and willful falsification carries severe penalties."

On December 6, a postal card, DSS Form 201, arrived directing us to appear at Abraham Lincoln School on December 10 for a blood test. The days were moving swiftly, because on December 21 came DSS Form 57, our notice of classification, 1–A. We always wondered how this could be given in spite of having had only a blood test. They knew we were breathing and had red blood, apparently!

On January 12, 1943, came DDS Form 150, "Greetings From the President of the United States," ordering us to report again at the Abraham Lincoln School at 7 a.m. on Thursday, January 21, "for the purpose of determining your availability for training and service in the Armed Forces of the United States." How thoughtful of the Rochester Transit Corp.! They provided several of their new automatic-transmission buses, which had arrived two months previously, to drive us to the Induction Station, situated in the basement of the Federal Building on Church Street (now City Hall). It was still dark when we arrived there.

Our group of 150 men from Irondequoit and Rochester

spent about four hours in physical and mental examinations. There were some with whom we were graduated from Irondequoit High School a mere 19 months previously, including Don Hess and Chet Turner.

At noon, the group walked to the Powers Hotel for lunch. Don't ask what we were served; the excitement was too much at that point! On returning to the Induction Station an hour or so later, we were sworn in, promising "to bear true faith and allegiance to the United States—to serve them honorably and faithfully against all their enemies, foreign and domestic, and to obey the orders of the President of the United States and the officers appointed by Congress, according to the Rules and Articles of War." Heavy stuff!

The small orchestra of Frank Monk, which was featured on WHAM's *Hank & Herb* program, provided music and one number played was "When the Lights Go On Again, All Over the World." That time seemed so far away to us. Monk had the saddest look on his face, as if he were sorry for all of us. The Induction Center commandant, Major Llewellyan Lloyd, then told us we were in the "greatest army in the world," and a First Sergeant with a chest of decorations advised us on the future. We couldn't miss!

Our attitude at that moment? It was a feeling of calm resignation. As one who shies from procrastination as much as possible, it was a relief to know where we stood. We were in "excellent physical condition" though 20 pounds underweight and we were in the Army, period. The point of no return had been reached. Furthermore, we believed that service to one's country could be a personal achievement, and a good segment of one's life on which to reflect later.

We were given Special Order No. 273, which transferred us from active duty to the enlisted reserve, and under jurisdiction of Board 558 for one week to enable us to settle our personal affairs.

On Thursday, January 28, 1943, we departed from Ridgewood School for the New York Central Station (again in one of the newest RTC buses) from whence we entrained at 10:30 a.m. for Fort Niagara and 34 months as EM 32675872.

Upon arriving in Buffalo, we had lunch in New York Central's big dining room. The menu? Forget it! We sure did! (A couple months ago, we visited the ghostly station, trying to envisage just where we ate. It had to be a cavernous main floor room which is now deserted and receives only basic maintenance).

We were then bused to Fort Niagara and assigned to one of the old two-story brick barracks, adjacent to the parade ground. To wind up a very eventful day, we were given the Army's Intelligence Test that evening. Getting to bed around midnight, we were rudely aroused five hours later, by a bugle's being blown into a megaphone nearby, and ushered outside into the sub-freezing weather to stand roll call.

Oh, yes. Our pay for those early days in the service was $50 a month, which was considerably more than the $21 a month which the draftees of 1940 received.

It was quite an experience, especially for one who had never been away from home alone in his life. In 34 months, we saw much of the United States, Alaska and the Aleutian Islands. Would we care to do it again? Only if our talents could be better utilized than they were 33 years ago. Specialized training in chemical warfare enabled us to become a Chemical NCO. Our previous occupation as a bank clerk certainly didn't qualify us for our Army position!

But there is one comforting thought: We served in the last war which this country legally entered and with the goal of winning.

EARLY ROCHESTER RADIO

February 1976

Local radio, before television's arrival in the late forties, had some great "live" programs, but how many Irondequoiters know that radio in this area had its beginnings in our town and employed a number of town residents in its development?

Prior to 1917, Lawrence G. Hickson built one of the state's largest wireless installations at his home on Ridge Road in Irondequoit. It had to be dismantled when the country entered World War I, but after the Armistice, Hickson resumed operations. On December 2, 1920, in his home on East Parkway, the area's first broadcast of music was heard. Recordings were used.

In 1922, he sold the equipment to publisher Frank E. Gannett, whose newspaper offices were located in the old Times-Union Building. In 1925, Hickson set up a transmitter in the rear of his store at 36 South Ave. with studios in the Seneca Hotel, the initials of the Hickson Electric Co. becoming a part of the new station's call letters—WHEC. Later, the transmitter was moved to the Terminal Building for greater range; in 1929, the station was housed in the new Rochester Savings Bank Building, 40 Franklin St. It is now on East Ave.

In 1922, the Gannett Newspapers presented transmission equipment to the Eastman School of Music. It eventually became the Stromberg-Carlson "50,000-watt, hi-fidelity, clear-channel station WHAM," with studios in the Sagamore Hotel on East Ave. Until WSAY became a third station in the thirties, WHAM and WHEC competed in Rochester. And what programs originated from their studios! Those were the days of live shows, live musicians and live actors!

Beginning in 1934, there was a Boy Scout news program on WHAM. Prefaced with the salutation "Good afternoon, Scouts and Scouters," Walter E. Hastings (Hubbs & Hastings Paper Co. executive) told of Camp Cory, Courts of Honor, new troops, etc. Interspersing live music was a brilliant young pianist, Syl Novelli. Novelli, now director of public relations for the Rochester Chamber of Commerce, still provides piano stylings in the smart clubs in the area while leading his orchestra. "Walter was synonymous with scouting in this area, and a great personal friend of mine," says Syl. "It was a shock to learn of his death."

The Major and the Minor utilized the two-piano arrangements of Helen Ankner and Clyde Morse in the late twenties. Miss Ankner was associated with local radio for many years, having other programs aired over WHAM. Morse also served as WHAM program director.

Frank Monk and His Merry Music Makers furnished music for WHAM's *Hank & Herb Show* and *The Kendall Houseparty.* The latter show in 1940–41 featured a variety of talent, including Jane and Carl, the *Sunshine Pals;* Bradley Kincaid, the *Kentucky Mountain Boy;* accordionist Beaney Morgan and MC Foster Brooks. (Yes, the same Foster who has become the lovable drunk on TV). Morgan and Brooks were the principals on WHAM's *Sunrise Special* each weekday morning. Theme: *Camptown Races.*

Through the first three decades of local radio, we had an abundance of music and songs provided by these remembered performers: Irene Gedney, Sax Smith and His Cavaliers, Ken Sparnon's Streamliners, Norbert Klem, Justin Conlon, Carl

Sax Smith and His String Orchestra were featured over Rochester's WHAM in 1930. From left: Sax Smith, Jack DeWitt, Alfred Monk, Norbert Klem, and Bob Hemmings.

Dengler (still going strong after 50 years as a bandleader and drummer), Charles Siverson's WHAM orchestra, Art Steffen (singing *Songs for You*), Nicholas Pagliara, Dick Hull, Hugh Dodge, Al Heckman, Edward C. May, J. Gordon Baldwin, Jerry Vogt, Max Rainey and his Hi-Boys with Flossie, Si Hall, Sparky Gillan and Vern Allen; Herbie Zahn, Tommy Thomas, Henry Freeman, Bob Hemmings and Gene Zacher.

One of the most popular dramatic programs was "True Stories of the New York State Police," first on both stations, then a Thursday night fixture on WHAM. Wayne Shoemaker researched material from State Police files, wrote the scripts, directed and acted. Cast regulars included Jack Lee, Gene Lane, William Fay, Hazel Coles, Mary Louise Taggart, Joseph Shale, and Dick Toole.

Not to be forgotten either was WHAM's *Hank & Herb* show on Saturday nights at 7, later 6:30. Also called *The Old Timers,* it starred Jack Lee (chief announcer) and Gene Lane in the title roles. This half-hour program which began in 1932 and ran for about 10 years, was a must as we howled to the antics of the operators of Higgins & Hoopers Filling Station and the Alert Towing Service, constable "Cheese & Crackers'" Jenkins, the widow Martha, the dog "Cyclone", etc. Sponsor was Widmer's Wine Cellars of Naples, N.Y.

One of the pioneers in play-by-play baseball broadcasting was WHEC's Gunnar Wiig, who had a voice which was not only distinctive, but it carried as well. ("It's going higher, higher, and it's over the fence for a home run and a case of Wheaties! Whoopie!") Every kid who heard him was impersonating Gunnar, the first voice of the Red Wings and an Irondequoit resident for a time. Others who came along in the same role, but never achieved the popularity were Harry McTigue, Garnet Marks, Jack Barry, Al Sisson, Addison Penfield, Ed Edwards and Jack Buck.

Sports news was ably covered daily by Al Sisson, Bill Rogers, Lowell MacMillan, Bob Turner and Carl Chamberlain, to name several.

Head and shoulders above all news announcers in popularity was amiable, folksy, Al "Howdy, Neighbors" Sigl, "old gravel voice", as he was affectionately known. He was a fixture on WHEC, direct from the Times-Union newsroom for over 35 years. So great was the man's common touch that he could ask for items for those in dire need, and before he left the air, his followers turned the Times-Union switchboard into a Christmas tree. An inveterate pipe-smoker, Al would sometimes get a coughing spell over the air and dismiss it by saying, "Well, that was a doozie, wasn't it?"

Though Al edited a column *Look & Listen* in the Saturday Times-Union tabloid section with the advent of television in 1947, he was always a radio personality. Al lived in Irondequoit for a number of years.

Other prominent news announcers and commentators were William Fay, Ken Loysen, Lew Stark, Harry LeBrun and Ken French (the Tydol News Reporters), Fritz Brownell (Tomorrow's Headlines), B. S. Bercovicci, Charlie Welch, Bill Despard, Roger Goodrich, Bill DeMarse, Ralph Knox, David E. Kesser, Howard Hosmer, and Jack Ross. And to err in the early years while reading a script was a rarity. You had to read accurately and you reviewed the script before going on the air!

Ladies' programs included *Mrs. Thriftybuyer;* the Sibley Tower Clock program with Carmen Ogden and music by Tom Grierson at the RKO Palace Wurlitzer; the IGA show with Mr. Iga; *Odds & Ends* with Bess Perry (Knope); and *To The Ladies* with Margot Gram who played her theme on the piano, *Tie A Little String Around Your Finger.*

The kiddies weren't overlooked when live radio had

something for everyone. In the early thirties, Santa Claus appeared daily for a week or two before Christmas to read letters sent to him at WHAM. *Aunt Mabel* was a WHEC favorite, reading stories to the children. Another was WHEC favorite *Young Stars of Tomorrow* on Sundays for years. First sponsored by Lobel's, then Stephen's children's apparel stores, the show had announcers who could put talented moppets at ease: Morden Buck, Frank Owen and Eddie Meath. Carl Piarulli, Jerry Vogt and Dick Hull accompanied those who "wanted to say hello to mom and dad, grandpa and grandma and everyone else listening in," following their routines.

Howard Severe MC'd WHEC's *Junior Town Meeting,* which involved high school students' discussions on issues of the day, and *Junior Quizdown* in which the intelligensia of the grade schools competed for sets of encyclopedias. *The Professor and His Brain Twisters,* with Morden Buck as MC, was an adult quiz show on WHEC in 1936–37 and *The Quiz of Two Cities* (Rochester and Buffalo) with Jack Barry was popular on Sunday afternoons before World War II on WHEC.

There were ethnic programs, too. *Melodies of Poland,* MC'd by Irondequoiter Ed Katafiaz, was a Sunday afternoon feature of WHEC for years. The Italian-American program, with Attillio Iachelli, was the longest sustaining live program in the city. In the thirties, Otto Stern and Ernie Stem "We play for you a *marsh!*" led the Bavarian Peasant Orchestra over WHAM, direct from the Pittsford Inn, the building which now houses offices of Wolfe Publications Inc. The area lost something when these programs left the air. Canned music can't hold a candle to live shows.

We hope that we have twitched the memories of those who lived through the glorious era of local radio. And Irondequoit residents had a big part in the local evolution of "The Opiate of the Masses."

DOOR-TO-DOOR SALESMANSHIP

April 1976

The days of most of the hucksters and door-to-door salesmen were numbered by the advent of World War II. There are relatively few left, and these are outnumbered by the fund-drive solicitors and advocates of "good causes."

The fact that there are ordinances requiring licenses for these people is a good factor in efforts to keep them at a minimum.

Time was when hardly a day or two passed when one wasn't visited by a huckster, salesman, deliveryman or pitchman. For example, before mechanical refrigeration, an almost daily visit by the iceman was a way of life. You'd place a card in your front window, its position indicating whether you wanted 25, 50, 75 or 100 pounds. "The iceman cometh," either by horsedrawn wagon or truck.

Our deliveryman, Mr. Hanke, had a bright red Ford Model T, labeled *Glendale Ice Co.* There was always the cleanup after the dripping block was dropped into the ice box. And on hot days, there were the inevitable kids who jumped onto the vehicle's back step for small chunks of ice to chew.

Fruit and vegetable hucksters were common, first with horse-drawn rigs, usually with a bright umbrella over the driver's seat. Later, of course, came trucks with canopies to give the merchandise some protection from the elements. A pyramid affair was built into the truck body, so the baskets and boxes of produce could be displayed.

The inevitable scale swung nearby and empty baskets swung between the wheels. The last produce huckster who visited our area of Irondequoit was a Charles F. Payne, who drove a bright yellow Ford truck. We believe he went out of business before World War II.

There were door-to-door men for all purposes. One had a motor bike with a power takeoff to run a grinding wheel. He went thru the neighborhoods, ringing a bell to announce he was available to sharpen knives and repair umbrellas.

Periodically, a junk man made his rounds, buying bundles of newspapers, bags of rags, old boilers, bed springs, metal, etc. Sitting on his horse-drawn wagon, he'd shout "Rags, papers, junk!" The housewives bargained with these fellows for better prices.

There were butter-and-egg men, too. One stopped at our house every Monday morning with a two-pound crock of fresh creamery butter, a change bag hanging on a strap around his neck. The price? Would you believe 50 cents for two pounds?

Magazine salesmen were prolific. "I'm working my way through college," was a common pitch. You could subscribe to a couple dozen magazines: *Saturday Evening Post, Literary Digest, Collier's, Liberty, Better Homes & Gardens, Girls' Life, American Boy, Boys' Life, Popular Mechanics, Popular Science, Women's Home Companion, Parents Magazine,* etc. One salesman parked his car near the school we attended and talked boys into becoming salesmen. A real glib pitchman!

There was a chap who made his rounds, identifying himself: "I'm Mr. Musicus. I'm a private music teacher." Happened he was also selling musical instruments such as accordions, which were very popular then.

When ice was delivered to your home before the motor truck, a burly "iceman cometh" in a wagon drawn by massive draft horses. A portion of the Rochester Ice & Cold Storage Utilities fleet is shown in Maplewood Park.

Another came around with the pitch, "Have you any old suits of clothes? I give top prices." Yes, things were a bit rough in the years of the Great Depression before a war economy pulled us out of it.

There were the inevitable Fuller Brush men and one could tell they worked on commission. They employed the "hard sell" and many housewives would buy a hair brush or comb just to get rid of the men who were "working their way through" or "have a family to support." They were the most persistent of salesmen.

There were men who sold only brooms and brushes and usually had a huge number they lugged around. On a hot day it must have been very tiring for these poor souls, bowed by the weight of their merchandise.

Once a year, often in the spring, representatives from the major photo studios toured the area, offering a "sensational offer" in portraits, especially at homes with children. Agents from Mock, Morrall, Moser and Rogers gave coupons, which meant savings off the regular price if the bargains were executed in 30 or 60 days.

Even though there are ice cream hucksters today, the present Skippy or Frosty Teddy outfits don't have the appeal of the rigs of yore. A brightly painted (usually white with red trim) horse-drawn wagon was used, the driver ringing a bell and shouting, "ice cream!" Whenever the kids gathered, the wagon stopped and the operator filled cones, or if you wanted a dishful, you'd provide him with one to fill. There was no ready packaging then, no ice cream on a stick. A metal scoop was dipped into containers of ice cream, surrounded with dry ice.

At the height of the Depression, there were the inevitable salesmen with small items, such as pencils, needles, thread, etc. Some of them appeared on their last legs, and it was pitiful the way they tried to keep body and soul together. Perhaps "beggars" would most aptly describe them. These people were one of the barometers of the Depression: the deeper it became, the more profuse they were—and desperate.

One came to our house one day, saying "I'm selling pencils and I suppose you hope I don't sell any." Mother's reply was, "Well, you certainly have an odd approach for one who's trying to sell something!"

One of the best known door-to-door outfits were the Wehle Baking rigs. Painted a bright yellow with interiors of white, the horse-drawn affairs had drawers and shelves for all varieties of baked goods. The housewife placed a yellow card on which was a red "W" in her window if she wanted anything, and the route man would stop, bringing in a tray of goodies.

When the firm was taken over by the House of Hathaway, the wagons were modernized by installation of rubber tires and repainting. The event was observed on our street when the route man, Looie, gave the kids a ride (all the way to the corner) on his refurbished wagon.

Another bakery was Town Talk of Pullman Avenue in the city, but it didn't have the prestige or common touch of Wehle. Deliveries were made with small Ford panel trucks.

In those days, your milk was delivered in bottles from dairies such as Bartholomay, Plymouth, Kort's, Brighton Place, Schreiner's, Hudson, Weber's, etc., at 11 cents a quart! Wagons were used in summer, sleighs in winter. Later, of course, came the trucks.

The Cook Coffee Co. and Jewel Tea Co. also made their rounds with small panel trucks. Cook is still in business, and one occasionally sees their trucks serving stores.

An era slowly ended with the demise of the huckster, door-to-door salesman and deliveryman. Now, most everyone satisfies his needs in shopping plaza supermarket stores, not far from home.

VARIED CRAFT ON LAKE ONTARIO

June 1976

Power-driven craft have always been a source of interest to us, whether it's a grimy tugboat or a massive ocean-going vessel. In the thirties, one could sit on the Summerville breakwater and see a greater variety of ships and boats than he sees today. And when the Canada's Cup Races were held, a kaleidoscope of watercraft was visible for miles on Lake Ontario off the Port of Rochester.

At 9:15 a.m. and approximately 12 hours later, a beautiful white-hulled car ferry steamed majestically between the piers. To us it was a thrilling experience to see this massive craft. In later years, we've seen ships several times the size of *Ontario I* and *Ontario II,* though not as thrilling.

For decades, Rochester was linked to several Canadian ports by three side-wheeler night boats of the Canada Steamship Lines: the 339-berth *Toronto,* built in 1899; the 365-berth *Kingston,* built in 1900, and the *Noronic. The Toronto* ran for 25 years under CSL aegis and was withdrawn from service in 1938 for reasons of weak boilers and objection of American authorities to her wooden main deck.

The *Kingston,* booked to capacity for her three-trip-a-week summer schedule, continued in service until the spectacular burning of the *Noronic* in 1949. The Canadian authorities adopted stricter fire-prevention measures and to keep the *Kingston* in service would have required an expenditure of $600,000 for fire-proofing. Not having the funds, the service was terminated.

The last of a long line of small steamers to run between Sea Breeze and Charlotte were the twin craft named *Sea Breeze 1* and *Sea Breeze 2,* operated for the Fix Bros. of Buffalo by Capt. Fred A. Roscoe of Sodus. When both were running, each ship would leave from a terminal, pass in the lake, and arrive at its destination. Departures were every hour. When the Depression cut into the excursion business, one ship was used.

One Sunday, while berthed at the end of Beach Avenue near the line's ticket booth in Charlotte, the *Sea Breeze 2's* boiler blew. The damage was repaired and the ship stayed in service. But its days were numbered. When both boats were retired, the dock at Sea Breeze was allowed to succumb to the ravages of the elements, and it was only a few years ago that the last pilings rotted away. The white and green ticket booth at Charlotte remained for a few years, serving the owners of a passenger launch, the *Rex,* which ran hourly trips into the lake and back just prior to World War II. Then, it too, disappeared.

The New York Naval Militia had an ex-submarine chaser, the wooden SC-433, berthed at Summerville at its Armory dock. A narrow-hulled vessel, built for speed, it was used for training reservists. It was always seen at special events such as the Canada's Cup Races and the annual Rochester Yacht Club's Fleet Review on Memorial Day. It had arrived here in 1922 with local reservist Ensign Benjamin Forsyth in charge of the crew. In January 1938, it was retired from service and sunk by depth charges seven miles northeast of the Charlotte lighthouse, the first United States naval craft to be scrapped in fresh water.

The Summerville Coast Guard Station had several vessels in

The *Sea Breeze I* steams up the river in September 1928. It was the last of many steamers on the Charlotte-Sea Breeze run.

the thirties. One was the *Eagle,* a cutter which eventually saw naval service in World War II. Two others were the *Forward* and the *Jackson.* There was the CG-2280, a grey-painted patrol boat which was used daily in rescuing sailors, towing disabled craft, etc. A beautiful white, broad-beamed picket boat with gleaming brass fixtures was pressed into service when the other units were on call. Capt. Mason B. McCune was the officer in charge, with second in command, Clifford Cronk.

In the spring, the U.S. Corps of Engineers had a dredge working in the river as far as the Genesee Docks to deepen the river to 23 feet. The *Taylor* had this chore for years until succeeded by the *Lyman.*

The Rochester Yacht club had a great variety of pleasure craft, even during the throes of the Depression. Perhaps the most stately was the *Kee Lox IV,* owned by carbon paper and ribbon king, Winifred B. Pembroke. It was a beautiful diesel-powered cruiser with a white hull. The boast by the owner was that the craft was "the first in and last out," meaning it was always the first craft at the Yacht Club to hit the launching ways in the spring and the last to be pulled out in the fall.

The Van Voorhis family of Irondequoit had an impressive black-hulled sailing ship. If memory serves, Judge J. Webb L. Sheehy has had the *Neeaga* for many years. It dates back to the twenties, if not before. The *Over 'n Back* was a cabin cruiser owned by Dr. Raymond Elliott. James Williams owned the sleek cruiser *Phyllis II.* Publisher Frank E. Gannett's yacht was the *Widgeon,* a favorite mecca for kids whenever they happened in the yacht club's basin. There were many more.

One of those who berthed their craft at a Genesee River slip was Oliver Kingsland, Jr., owner of the *Yum-Yum.* This inboard, built in his father's garage on Long Acre Road in Irondequoit, had an airplane engine, and the hull was especially reinforced to handle greater stress. Even so, the prow rose high out of the water, due to torque, when maximum speed was applied. Oliver's father had a more conventional inboard and his brother-in-law Howard Buhlmann had an outboard craft, both also built in the Long Acre Road garage.

When the Canada's Cup Yacht Races were held for 8–meter boats, every three or four years, the event brought out everyone—a real carnival atmosphere along the lake. Landlubbers, armed with binoculars, lined the two piers. Boats of every description, from canoes to car ferries, dotted the waters of Lake Ontario. Who can forget *Thisbe,* sailed by clothing company executive William P. Barrows, which defeated the Canadian *Quest* in 1930. Or the *Conewago,* skippered by Wilmot V. "Rooney" Castle, the winner over the Canadian *Invader II,* captained by Norman Gooderham, a few years later. Official observation boats for the races were the aforementioned *Ontario I* and *Ontario II,* each able to accomodate 1,000 onlookers.

There were craft which visited Rochester also. In 1928, the British convict sailing ship, *Success,* over 125 years old, showed 8,000 visitors at Charlotte what it was like to be a prisoner in the 18th Century at sea. A "Floating Devil's Island" would have been an appropriate term for this craft as it displayed such appurtenances as leg irons, torture devices, iron cages, etc.

Before World War II, a former U.S. Navy submarine, which was on a tour of the Great Lakes ports, tied up at Charlotte, and for 25 cents one could see what a cramped vessel it was. It was indeed a far cry from the modern nuclear-powered undersea craft which can remain on station for months at a time.

Yes, a trip to the lakeside in the Halcyon Days was an experience for a lover of boats. There are still many private craft which abound the waters, but the variety is not as great as it was 50 years ago.

The outer lobby of the RKO Palace Theatre a few weeks before it closed in 1965. Razing of "Rochester's Most Beautiful Theatre" was the crime of the decade.

A BLONDE CASHIER
A VASE OF ROSES

July 1976

Remember when going to the movies constituted a real experience? When you felt after two or three hours in a motion picture palace that you'd really been someplace? You got your money's worth and at popular prices, too! We're sure that many of the area's citizens will enjoy a nostalgic trip to the movie theatre of yesteryear.

When motion pictures were coming into their own and gaining more public support in the twenties because of great films, the era of the Motion Picture Palaces or "cathedrals" as they liked to call them, blossomed in America. These ornate structures were situated from coast to coast—from the sumptuous 6,214-seat Roxy in New York, to the grandiose 5,650-seat Fox in San Francisco.

The idea, and apparently it was a good one, was that people living in modest flats and cold-water tenements could, for 25 or 50 cents, go into a palace. So when they went to the movies, they went to places which created the total overwhelming feeling of escape. Usually, they were the first places in town to be air-conditioned ("air-cooled," they called it on simulated icicles adorning the marquees); they had footmen out front with umbrellas on rainy nights; and in the box office, the cashier had to be a blonde and there had to be a vase of roses.

There were two major styles of theatre architecture. One was the "atmospheric," created by an Austrian architect, John Eberson. The idea, as he put it, was to "put the audience into a magnificent amphitheatre under a glorious moonlit sky, where friendly stars twinkled and wisps of clouds floated by." The stars did twinkle and the clouds did float, projected onto the ceiling and constantly moving.

In one theatre, there was a notice to the staff: "Do not turn on the clouds until the show starts; turn off the stars when you leave."

The second style of theatre architecture was developed by Thomas Lamb and known as "the money style." He created "temples of gold, pageantry of Oriental splendor, creating an atmosphere in which the mind is free to frolic." He admitted that they were not architecturally perfect in some respects, but they did cause the ticket buyers' eyes to bulge. That they surely did!

"Traditional architects" called all the rococo, glint and glitter of these places laughable, and one, upon examining the new Loew's Kings Theatre in Booklyn, labeled it "An Indo-Persian-Sino-Egyptian-Byzantine-Romanesque monstrosity." But the public liked it and responded to the advertisements to "take the grand marble stairway to a seat in an acre of paradise."

In Rochester, as far as this writer was concerned, there was but one motion picture palace, and only one—the 2900-seat RKO Palace Theatre on Clinton Avenue North near Mortimer Street. There were other houses with good appointments, but none approached the Palace in sheer beauty and grandeur. After purchasing his ticket at the ornate box office, the patron walked into the outer lobby, adorned with large mirrors, crystal chandeliers and gold filigrees. Giving his ticket to the uniformed attendant, he then entered the grand foyer, replete with more mirrors, gold leaf, chandeliers, paintings and red velvet tapestries. If the auditorium were full, patrons waited behind shiny stanchions, connected with red velvet retainers. You sunk in carpeting up to your ankles.

Upon entering the auditorium, having more of the same colors and decor, plus gilt chandeliers, gold organ grilles, and rich contour stage curtains, the patron was guided to his seat by a uniformed usher where he witnessed the show in a plush upholstered chair in a climate-controlled atmosphere.

That's the way it was when we were theatre-going in the early thirties. The Palace had a pit orchestra, "The RKOlians," directed by Russ Kahn. It played the overture and accompanied the six acts of top-grade vaudeville. A typical bill may have included a singer, some dancers, a juggler, a wire act, a magician, and a balancing-dog act. Famous personalities trod the Palace's boards on their way to stardom: Bob Hope, Morton Downey, Kate Smith, Harry Blackstone, among others.

Following the vaudeville, the newsreel, a cartoon and announcement of coming events, came the feature picture, and there were great ones in those days: *The Dawn Patrol* with Richard Barthelmess; *Captain January* with Guy Kibbee and Shirley Temple; *Dirigible* with Jack Holt; *Treasure Island* with Wallace Berry and Jackie Cooper; *Chained* with Clark Gable and Joan Crawford; *Mutiny on the Bounty* with Charles Laughton and Clark Gable; *King Kong* with Fay Wray, Robert Armstrong and Bruce Cabot; and several Fred Astaire/Ginger Rogers pictures.

After the movie, the filmy scrim was drawn across the screen, the contour curtain was dropped, and a golden spotlight swung to the left of the orchestra pit to pick up a white and gold organ console as it slowly rose to the tune of the thunderous

"RKO March". At the controls of the Mighty Wurlitzer was Tom Grierson, whose name became synonymous with theatre organ playing in Rochester. He'd present a couple solos and, talking into a carbon microphone, enlisted the audience's efforts in a sing-along, the curtains having parted again for the words to be projected on the screen. To vary the routine, he'd ask the men to sing, then the ladies, then all together for the finale. Tom had great rapport with his followers. On weekday mornings, he broadcast from the Palace over WHAM on Sibley's *Tower Clock* program, which was preceded by actual street sounds and the Sibley Tower's chimes.

The great era of the motion picture palace faded after World War II. The electronic boxes we have in our living rooms, called TV sets, were responsible. Vaudeville was gone and so were the newsreels. Use of pipe organs and orchestras in theatres was limited to a handful of such prestigious houses, such as the Radio City Music Hall in New York. A new wave of realism swept into pictures as well. Small, intimate theatres were more suited to sophisticated films than theatres with cavernous interiors. And above all, pressures of economics helped seal the doom of most of these palaces of pleasure.

It was a sad day when wreckers' axes tore into the RKO Palace in 1965. "Rochester's Most Beautiful Theatre" was on the way to oblivion, it, too, the victim of steadily rising costs and changes in people's entertainment habits. The Wurlitzer was saved and installed in the Auditorium Theatre by the Rochester Theater Organ Society, so one aspect of the Palace lives on through monthly concerts from September through May by leading theatre organists.

But the memories of our attending shows at the Palace in the thirties and forties are still vivid and every time we pass the site of the magnificent theatre, we have twinges of sorrow, if not the pangs of anger, because of its destruction. It was the crime of the decade when that great theatre was razed, thereby depriving Rochester of a Performing Arts Center with perfect acoustics and complete equipment for every conceivable type of presentation.

In 1930, about 90 million went to the movies every week; today the figure is much less. In 1930, there were 23,000 movie palaces; today there are perhaps a couple hundred, and they are still coming down. Taking their places are parking lots, office buildings and supermarkets; but not one has a gilt chandelier, a mighty Wurlitzer, or a grand stairway to paradise.

A rare view of the two Ontario car ferries. *Ontario I* (rt.) has swung into position to pull her sister ship from the sandbar off Crescent Beach in March 1936.

ROCHESTER TO COBURG VIA CAR FERRY

August 1976

It was always a thrill when we happened to be near the lakeshore at Charlotte about 8:30 p.m. during the thirties and forties. A smudge of soft coal smoke appeared on the northwest horizon; then, pin-pointed with lights, came the white superstructure of a massive, broad-beamed vessel. One of the Ontario car ferries was steaming majestically to her destination, the Genesee Docks. It was a sad day when these great vessels ended their 43 years of service from Rochester to Coburg, Ontario, Canada.

In 1907, the Buffalo, Rochester & Pittsburg Railway concluded an agreement with Canada's Grand Trunk Railroad, creating the Ontario Car Ferry Co. Ltd., which resulted in the building of the Ontario I. This vessel made its first trip to Rochester on November 15, 1907. Three years later, the Rochester & Pittsburgh Coal and Iron Co., a BR&P subsidiary, built at a cost of $200,000, a high steel coal trestle at the Genesee Docks, situated along the Genesee River at Boxart Street. This facility was used by colliers exclusively.

In 1915, Ontario II entered service. A boat train, running from the BR&P station on West Main Street to the docks in the morning and returning after the ferry's arrival in the evening, was instituted for passengers.

The ferries, which were registered in Montreal, were of the same size and design. Only the pilot houses at the stern were different. Each was steel-hulled, twin-screw propelled, 4100 tons, 316 feet long, 54 feet wide, of 3500 HP, and had a capacity of 1,000 passengers and 28 hopper cars of coal. The ships' prime function was to haul coal to Canada. The trip took about five hours, plus two hours spent in Coburg as the cars of coal were removed and empties substituted for the return trip. Two well known captains were Charles E. Redfearn and Samuel McCaig.

Though mostly routine, the ferries' history was spotted with newsmaking events. Once while enroute to Canada, a carload of coal got free and rolled off the rear of the vessel. Somewhere, there are 40 tons of bituminous on Lake Ontario's bottom.

In 1918, both ships were held in ice floes off the Port of Rochester. In 1928, *Ontario II,* while turning at the Genesee Docks, was forced by the strong current into a mud bank. Locomotives and a tug could not free her, so her sister ship came from Coburg and pulled her off. In 1933, *Ontario II* grounded on a sandbar in Coburg harbor. On February 9, 1934, *Ontario II* stuck in the ice of Charlotte Pier. It was the area's coldest day in recorded history, 22 below zero. Veteran Times-Union newsman, Abe Miller, was sent to the ship for a story of its imprisonment and stayed overnight, reporting that the ship was never in any danger. During the 58 consecutive hours of sub-zero cold, Lake Ontaro was frozen clear across, and in Captain Redfearn's words, "A dog could have walked across if he avoided the air holes." Many people, including the writer, went for a "walk on Lake Ontario," some venturing beyond the lighthouses.

In 1936, *Ontario II* again provided newspaper copy for

almost a week as she went aground on a sandbar off Crescent Beach. Her sister ship again was summoned to pull her off, something the Coast Guard cutter *Jackson* could not do, even with shifting of her cargo of wood pulp at high tide.

But on Friday night, September 7, 1934, *Ontario I* provided the most memorable but near disastrous event. Five hundred passengers were aboard for a moonlight cruise on the lake, sponsored by a local restaurateur, Joe Ryan. The sea was a bit heavy with rain falling. About 11:30, the ship lurched violently when it was turned around. Tables, chairs, cauldrons of soup, passengers, anything not fastened, slid violently about. The result was near panic. Captain Redfearn wirelessed for aid from the Coast Guard, and the cutter *Eagle* was dispatched to stand by. The *Eagle* asked for ambulances to meet the ship at the Genesee Docks, and a special Baltimore & Ohio train was rushed to bring the 60 injured to city hospitals.

At the inevitable hearing, the helmsman seemed to provide the answer to the near tragedy. He explained that "this sort of thing had happened before when there was a lack of cargo or ballast. The ship would bob about like a cork until riding out the swell, caused by her turning." Crew members always insisted that *Ontario I* seemed harder to manage than her sister craft.

This episode of car ferry history was a big event in the Rochester press, but on the same night, the Ward Line's coastal steamer, the *Morro Castle,* bound from Havana to New York, burned off Asbury Park, New Jersey, with a loss of 125 lives. There were fortunately no lives lost on the *Ontario I* incident, but there were over $400,000 in injury claims, which were settled after two years of litigation for $25,000.

Beginning in 1931 as the Great Depression deepened, one ferry was used in daily service, but the other could get steam up within hours if needed for rescue of its sister ship or for special excursions. In 1941, with increased war effort, both vessels were employed in daily service again and in 1941, because of minimal passenger service, the boat train to Charlotte was discontinued.

Following the war, ferry service declined again, and by February, 1950, only two or three trips a week were being made by *Ontario II.* The *Ontario I* had been offered for sale in August, 1949. On April 28, 1950, the *Ontario II* passed under the upraised Stutson Street Bridge, enroute to Canada for the last time, flags flying and its heavy doppel whistle honking. A few months later the ships were scrapped, the *Ontario I* in Humberstone, Ontario, the *Ontario II* in Port Dalhousie, Ontario. The high steel trestle at the Genesee Docks was dismantled in 1974. Only a dock of sufficient size to accomodate cement haulers exists as a reminder of the days which were.

In spite of the fact that Dad had a pass, enabling his family to travel free on the BR&P system, we never had the experience of a trip on the ferries. Thoughts of sea sickness were factors; and we have regretted since their passing, that we didn't take a trip, especially during the Canada's Cup Races. The ships were the official observation boats for these regattas in the twenties and thirties. In fact, one of the ferries aroused the ire of the judges in 1932 by steaming slowly between the judges' boat and the contenders to give her spectators a closer view!

However, in spite of periodic newsworthy events it was a grand era and the communities concerned lost something with the retirement of the white-hulled beauties.

DIM AND ANCIENT HALLS

September 1976

Old structures have a fascination for many. Aging theatres, churches, office buildings, stores, and schools can be sources of much sentimentality. For us, the pile of red brick which once stood at the northwest corner of Titus Avenue and Cooper Road, known as Irondequoit High School, will be forever enshrined in our memories.

After eight years in Hosea Rogers Grammar School (opened in 1929), it was a bit shocking to enter IHS the first time. Everything reeked of the past. The front portion was built in 1895, another section was added in 1908. In 1922, the school's size was more than doubled, and in 1927 two portables were attached. Old IHS, like Topsy, "just growed."

However, four years of toil were ahead of us as we climbed the six stone steps to the entrance on Tuesday morning, September 7, 1937. Wooden floors and stairways in the front section creaked with every step. Several layers of paint and varnish didn't encourage the establishment of smoking lounges!

Freshmen and sophomore rooms were on the second floor, junior and senior rooms on the first, with many students having their lockers in the basement. But in spite of the building's antiquity and the minor inconvenience of getting to one's locker between classes (the exercise was worth it), we had some very wonderful times in that old building—make no mistake about it!

Mr. Alfred C. Hamilton was principal of the school and superintendent of Dictrict 3, and when it was proposed in 1937 that he receive a raise to $4800 a year, what a howl went up in some areas! He was worth every penny. He ran a tight ship, was always at the bottom of the stairs as students raced to the basement cafeteria at noon, and while they were eating, he was a self-appointed overseer, making sure the lunch bags were properly deposited in trash cans, and the milk bottles in their wooden crates. Maybe Mr. Hamilton was not a born diplomat, but there was no discipline problem at IHS in those days.

The majority of students walked to school. A smaller number rode bicycles, which were housed in the basement on racks, a wooden ramp being used to move them in and out. A handful of students owned cars: Gordon Rambert drove an antique Buick; classmate Bruce Bertsch brought his friends to school in a rakish Hudson convertible. The few cars owned by students and teachers were parked on a small gravel area between the school and United Congregational Church.

If one couldn't attend school because of illness, a parent called Glenwood 412 and informed the authorities. Mr. Hamilton made his rounds during the first period, checking absentees listed on a pad in each home room, and if there were anyone not accounted for (such as Dick Kaiser who liked to stay home and build model airplanes), attendance officer Rudy Dietrich drove to the student's home for an explanation. Rudy also directed outside traffic at noon and at 3:05 p.m.

Assembly programs were held in the gymnasium, with Mr. Bell and his assistant, George Groom, setting up folding chairs. There were no upholstered seats in an air-conditioned auditorium! A football rouser was the first assembly in the fall, the students being made aware of "school spirit," by German teacher Harry Wagner. There were periodic film showings, speakers, and some programs given by students. We recall one by members of Mr. Wesley Graves' physics and chemistry classes which attempted to pass electricity through the student body which had joined hands. It didn't work beyond the first row!

Once in the fall and again in the spring, the National Honor Society held its "tapping" ceremony. Juniors and seniors who maintained marks in the 90–to-100 bracket and evincing qualities of leadership and service were rewarded by induction into the NHS. Members passed among the student body and tapped the inductees on the shoulder, signifying their entrance into the exclusive club of the brainy. No, folks, I was not one of the elite!

In June, the students gathered for the reading of the graduating class will and prophecy to the juniors who became seniors the following year. Once a year, the school, with its thin walls and ill-fitting doors, got the "sulphur treatment." The chemistry classes conducted an experiment involving this material, and the resulting odor permeated most of the old building. Mr. Graves and his successor, Carlton Jamieson, were classified as "stinkers" for the day! No oversize Airwicks then!

There were extracurricular clubs to serve varied interests at old IHS. The school paper, the *Rodequoit,* attracted those who interests were writing and other phases of journalism. The Orion Society was a magnet for would-be actors, providing a reservoir of talent for the National Honor Society play and the Senior play. There were the Visual Aid Corps, Sketch Club, Library Club, German Club, Airplane Club, French Club (Les Babillards), International Relations Club, Camera Club, Sports Club and Tri-Y.

Mr. and Mrs. Alfred C. Hamilton observe their 50th wedding anniversary in 1964. Principal of Irondequoit High School, he was also superintendent of School District 3.

The last-named organization, a girls' club, had a day when it initiated new members through all sorts of stunts and hi-jinks in zany regalia and painted faces. However, they were a dedicated group, serving people through worthwhile projects.

So, with athletics, clubs, and and chorus, there was hardly a student who didn't participate in at least one extra-curricular activity.

Of course, there were the inevitable pranks, perpetuated by those who didn't have enough to do! One always occurred during the spring thaw. The library, situated in one of the portables, had a sloping roof which resulted in some dandy icicles. Frequently, a tall student (invariably a male) opened a swing-out window, broke off an icicle, and deposited it on a chair. Being near a radiator, it melted quickly and a pool of water awaited a victim. Ever attend a class with a moist dorsal region? Very damp and squishy! Wonder if this ever happened to faculty members; they ate their lunches in the library.

Occasionally, students started sneezing repeatedly. Al Martin and his sneeze powder had struck again! One day in Mr. Richard Tefft's plane geometry class, he spotted something funny. In seconds, the entire class was in an uproar. One student, noticing a loose thread hanging from the sweater of a classmate seated ahead of him, started to pull it. A pile of red yarn grew on his desk! No wonder some of us barely scraped through that course!

And how about the times when general science teacher Warren "Pop" Pierson backed into a lighted Bunsen Burner he had hung on the wall some moments before? He would become so engrossed in lecturing on *The Factors of our Environment,* he had completely forgotten. Nothing like burning one's britches behind him, but it was always good for a roar of laughter.

One day there was evidence of a skunk which had been

trapped under one of the portables. What students missed in odor from the chemistry classes, was more than made up with the scent from this occurrence!

The new high school on Cooper Road was dedicated in 1950. The old structure was idle until a fire of "unknown origin" gutted it in 1951 and it was razed shortly after. The two portables which extended onto the athletic field (a yellow sign with black lettering read: "No hardball playing on these grounds, by order of Board of Education") were sold to a farmer for use as chicken coops. A bank now stands on the site.

But one cannot erase the fond memories of old IHS in which the Class of 1941 were handed their diplomas that humid Monday evening, June 23, 1941, by Mr. Hamilton and then marched out to Mendelsohn's *War March of the Priests,* played by the school's music director, Lawrence Parker. *Vendi, Vidi, Vici!*

TRACKLESS TROLLEYS

October 1976

Those who had occasion in the twenties and early thirties to use public transportation for a crosstown trip across the Driving Park Avenue Bridge, rode in a conveyance which was indigenous to that route. During the history of this vehicle, it has been known by several names: trolley coach, trolley bus, electric bus or trackless trolley. It was by the last designation that it was always identified in Rochester.

The idea for trackless trolleys here was apparently to see if they could operate profitably and efficiently on a short route by offering a medium of transfer with seven north-south trolley lines. During the hearings which were held prior to approval of the system, there were several points of opposition raised. One centered on whether the vehicles would be equipped with tire chains in the winter, which would cause havoc to the pavements, mostly brick.

Another questioned the stability of Driving Park Avenue Bridge. One opponent cited the Rae Oil Works fire in 1923 (burned for a week), when thousands using the obsolete Smith Street Bridge as a vantage point, were ordered off the structure because of the weight. However, City Engineer C. Arthur Poole assured everyone that the Driving Park Bridge was safe for the operation of the trackless trolleys.

A third protest was voiced by the 17th Ward Community

Club on the basis of the "objectionable features of the trackless trolley such as innumerable poles and overhead wires which would ruin the appearance of our streets and are dangerous as well as unsightly." The club favored gasoline-powered buses.

Objections or not, City Council awarded a franchise in 1923 to Rochester Railways' Co-ordinated Bus Lines. The unit was incorporated with $50,000 in capital stock. Commissioner of Railways Charles R. Barnes laid out the route. The western terminus was a loop at Driving Park Avenue and Pierpont Street and from there, the 2.78-mile line was through Driving Park Avenue, Avenue E., Conkey Avenue and Avenue D to a loop near Portland Avenue. Operation began at 6 a.m., October 16, 1923.

Five vehicles were initially purchased, but seven were added within a year. The chassis were built by the Brockway Motor Truck Company in Cortland, New York, and shipped to the

A new trackless trolley sans trolley poles, stands outside the St. Paul Street shops in 1923. Kodak's Hawk-Eye Works is in the background.

Kuhlman Car Company in Cleveland for body assembly. Painted green with cream trim, the vehicles seated 25 passengers, were 25 feet long, 7 feet wide, and had a swinging radius of 17 feet on either side of the trolley wires. Equipped with Overman "cushion tires," each trolley had a single front entrance-exit and was propelled by two 25 HP motors.

The four-wire overhead (two for each direction) was built at a cost of $8,850 per mile. Tubular steel poles, spaced 100 feet apart, supported the system.

Eventually, the New York State Railways bought out the stock of the Rochester Railways Co-ordinated Bus Lines, and the crosstown route became an integral part of the city transportation network. However, the subsidiary was kept a separate entity to determine profit-loss status and for other bookkeeping aspects.

According to one engineer, "the coaches operate over streets which, in most cases, would not be considered smooth. Most of the streets are narrow, of brick paving with many surface irregularities. Although the combination of rough streets and hard tires at first sounds like poor riding qualities, these coaches today could not be considered as rough riding."

Whom was he kidding? The trackless trolleys, riding over brick and cobblestone pavements, were real bouncing Bettys, and we know of one lady who was seriously injured when thrown against a stanchion as the vehicle stopped suddenly after a trolley pole left a wire. It resulted in a growth, which had to be eliminated by X-ray treatment.

In spite of the bumpy ride, the trackless trolleys did handle a good number of passengers. During the first nine months of 1928, for example, 1,149,202 were carried, while the mileage total was 186,210. This averaged to 37 passengers per round trip and 107 miles a day. A four-minute headway was maintained in rush hours, and a 12-minute headway in off-peak times.

Financial results were gratifying. Power and lubricant costs averaged 2.7 cents per car mile. Maintenance charges on poles, fixtures and overhead were $210.92 per mile in 1927.

In the late twenties, the gasoline-powered bus began to take over routes once dominated by the trolley car. Rochester was no exception: in 1929, the Plymouth Avenue car line was the first to be converted to buses. The idea behind this was that public transportation should be "freed from the shackles of tracks and overhead wires, thereby becoming more flexible." So, if a line employed tracks and wires, its days in Rochester were numbered.

The crosstown trackless trolleys bit the dust on March 3, 1932, being substituted by larger Mack gasoline-powered buses. Also, the crosstown route was changed later that year when the new Veterans Memorial Bridge was opened. However, there would be evidence of the trackless trolleys for some time after. One of the bodies served as a shelter at the Blossom Road trolley loop until vandals desecrated it. The body of TT No. 319 graced the Redder farm on Creek Street in Penfield for an even longer period, serving as a storage shed near the body of a Rochester & Syracuse trolley.

If one wishes to see trackless trolleys today, he must visit such disparate places as Seattle, San Francisco and Chicago. Atlanta once had more than any city in North America, 800. But, today's vehicles are a far cry from their ancient counterparts. They are noiseless, ride much smoother and are noticeably larger. Still, the ones we had in Rochester had an aura all their own; once you saw or rode them, the memories of them would always remain.

STADIUM ECHOES

April 1977

There have been some eventful times at 500 Norton Street, successively known as Red Wing Stadium and Silver Stadium. Those events will forever live in the memories of fans fortunate to have seen them in person or heard them over the radio.

The stadium opened in 1929. The Red Wings had become a Triple-A farm club of the St. Louis Cardinals the year before, and good talent passed through in copious supply. We recall attending a few games in the early 30s but were too young to remember details. This was when Albany was in the International League and featured a broad-beamed catcher by the name of "Shanty" Hogan. Now that goes back a bit!

Our awakening interest in the national pastime began about 1935 when Gunnar Wiig, the most famous play-by-play announcer in local history, was describing Red Wing games. In 1937, in company with several school companions, we attended a Knot Hole Gang event, played on a weekday afternoon. When Red Wing first baseman, Walter Alston, (later Dodger manager) hit a three-run homer, we were a fan for the duration.

It was the era of the great Newark teams. The Bears, a New York Yankee farm club, finished 25–1/2 games ahead of the pack in 1937. During a three-year period, the Bears sent to the majors such stars as these: Joe Gordon, Charlie Keller, Mike Chartak, Jimmy Gleason, Merril May, Hank Majeski, Ellsworth "Babe"

Dahlgren, Nolan Richardson, Frankie Kelleher, Buddy Rosar, Hank Borowy, Johnny Lindell, Joe Beggs, Willard Hershberger, Ed Levy, Bud Metheny and Tommy Holmes. It was the greatest collection of minor league talent in history.

But the Red Wings were the team which always gave the Bears the most trouble in season play. We had some pretty good players, too: Estel Crabtree, Jack Juelich, Johnny Hopp, Lou Scoffic, Jack Sturdy, Marty Marion, Phil Weintraub, Bob O'Farrell, "Nubs" Kleinke, Oscar Judd, Bill Walker, Sam Narron, Brusie Ogrodowski, Carden Gillenwater, Howard Krist, Si Johnson, Ken Raffensberger, Bob Bowman, Danny Murtaugh, Dusty Cooke, Mike Ryba, Whitey Kurowski, Harry Davis, George Fallon, Frank Crespi, Preacher Roe and Herschel Lyons.

Without doubt, the greatest single moment in Rochester baseball history occurred in September, 1939, when centerfielder Estel Crabtree with two out, two on base, and the team three runs behind in the ninth inning of the sixth game of the Shaughnessey

In 1940, the Red Wings won the pennant under three managers and an interim manager of one week. From left to right: Billy Southworth, Tony Kaufmann and Estel Crabtree. Pitcher Mike "Old Folks" Ryba was the interim pilot.

playoffs, hit one out of the park against the Bears' Norman Branch. Garnet Marks was broadcasting the game that Saturday evening, and in his excitement hollered: "If you don't support this Red Wing team, you're nuts!" Later, he tempered his outburst with an apology. No need! People who had departed the stadium, left their cars in the streets and returned to see the Wings win the game in the twelfth inning on Jim Asbell's hit. The following afternoon, before 16,000, the Wings, with Herschel Lyons pitted against Max Macon, beat Newark 2–1 to go into the Little World Series.

In the same season occurred the famous "foul ball" incident. In an evening game, Jack Sturdy skied one over the fence. "Foul," declared umpire Bill Kelly. To everyone in the park, including the opposing players, it was a fair ball. "What's the matter with Mr. Kelly?," asked Red Wing announcer Harry McTigue. Appeals were made to league president Frank Shaughnessey and the event was played up for days on radio and in the press. The decision stood, however.

In 1940, the Red Wings won their 10th pennant and under three managers. Billy Southworth started but was promoted to the Cardinals. His successor, Estel Crabtree, had a kidney operation and was succeeded by Tony Kaufman. But the team won, thanks to the superb pitching of Mike Ryba, Hank Gornicki, Herschel Lyons and Charley Brumbeloe, who accounted for 80 of the 96 games won by the team.

The following year was the last time the Wings finished in the first division for seven years. It was sparked by two late-season arrivals from the lower minors, Erv Dusak and Stan Musial, who proceeded to hit .304 and .326 respectively. Strangely, Dusak was the more highly touted of the pair, but Stan, promoted to the Cardinals at the end of the season, went on to re-write the major league record book, and achieve Hall of

Fame status. Dusak later was transferred back to Rochester as a pitcher, and eventually drifted out of baseball.

Wartime baseball saw players shuffled in and out of the Norton Street stadium like pawns in a chess game. Only one player stood out in that era: Albert "Red" Schoendienst. Dubbed "the team" by the late Times-Union baseball writer, Al Weber, Red went on to greatness in the majors after an army stint. But, a first-division berth for the Wings was out for the duration. In 1945, for example, there were 51 players, including 23 pitchers who wore Red Wing Flannels and somehow they managed to miss being killed by line drives, to the astonishment of the spectators.

After the war, baseball improved and the front office went out and got players. Hal Rice, for example, joined two Rochester players in the record books who batted in nine runs in a game: George "High Pockets" Kelly and James "Rip" Collins.

Two other players who excited the fans were Russell Alva Derry and Steve Bilko. Derry, who had seen wartime service with the Yankees, provided many a thrill with his long-distance clouts over the right field wall. So well liked here, he was presented a tractor for his Princeton, Missouri farm at the end of one season.

Bilko displayed awesome, raw power and fans still remember the Sunday afternoon when he powered five home runs in a double header. And they were hit to all fields. The Nanticoke Knocker's greatest enemy was his appetite, and after a brief period in the majors, principally with Detroit, he was out of baseball.

Outfielder Ed Mierkowicz was a great favorite, and those who saw his "beaning" still remember the sickening thud when the ball hit his head in a stadium game. It just about ended the Wyandotte, Michigan, resident's career.

Many fans still remember the 26–inning thriller between the Wings' Tom Poholsky and Jersey City's Andy Tomasic one Sunday. It ended when Dick Cole singled home third baseman, Don Richmond, as darkness descended. Another win for the Wings!

And what about the play-by-play broadcasters who paraded before the microphone through the years? Beginning with the most colorful, Gunnar Wiig, we've had Harry McTigue, Garnet Marks, Al Sisson, Jack Barry, Addison Penfield, Ed Edwards, Tom Decker, Jack Buck and Joe Culinane. How many of you remember a diminutive bat boy in the late 30's, Pee-Wee Juliano?

Before World War II, the Slager Post Band entertained on Sunday afternoons and holidays, and after the war, organ music was supplied by cigar-chomping Jimmy Kellogg.

There have been some memorable events, great players and colorful personnel at Red Wing (sorry, Silver) Stadium in the past 48 years. What will the next 48 years write into baseball history there?

Vincent DeRitis and Margay Roby prepare to board #55 at East Main barns. Operator William J. Whalen will guide the horse down Main to State to Edgerton Park, where the rig was to be featured in the "Pathways of Progress" pageant.

ROCHESTER CENTENNIAL

August 1977

The observance of Rochester's Centennial was a period of much celebration and pageantry. The bulk of festivities was held at Edgerton Park from August 11 to September 9, 1934, where a "Pathways of Progress" pageant was held.

The celebration was in preparation for months. Honorary Chairman for the Centennial was Mayor Charles Stanton; general chairman, Carl S. Hallauer; president, Harper Sibley; B. Emmett Finucane, Mrs. Richard T. Ford and Frank J. Smith, vice chairmen; treasurer, John A. Murray; secretary, Edward R. Foreman; and executive secretary, Roy R. Rumpff. Fifteen of the city's notables graced the executive committee.

Committees included general, finance, women's, pioneer, civic celebration, civic club, exposition and pageant, early Rochester, publicity and 24 others, 34 in all. The general committee boasted the largest membership, 121! In spite of the oversized groups, the affair ran surprisingly well.

One of the attractions at the pageant was horse car No. 55, which had been operated by the first transit system in the city, the Rochester City & Brighton Railroad. Discovered in a yard on Andrews Street, where it was being used as a playhouse, the New York State Railways acquired and completely refurbished it. At the East Main barns, the car was hitched to a horse, two young persons dressed in period costumes climbed aboard, deposited their nickles, and were off to Edgerton Park. William J. Whalen, who drove the car in the 1880s and was the oldest employee in point of service with the NYS Railways, manned the brakes and guided the reins. Made at the height of the noontime rush, the trip attracted many onlookers. After all, it was the first time since 1895 that a horse car was seen on the streets of Rochester. The vehicle is now part of the transportation museum at Riverton, New York.

Two wood-burning locomotives arrived to take their places in the pageant. One was the *De Witt Clinton* from the New York Central, the other was the *William Galloway* of the Baltimore & Ohio. They were officially received by railroad writer and historian, Edward Hungerford, who served as general chairman of the pageant and wrote the script of the ten-scene extravaganza.

There were other items of interest which made the pageant come alive. Antique fire apparatus was loaned by the Rochester and Brockport fire departments. The Towner Brothers provided old bicycles. A perambulator was made available by the Rochester Museum. Old automobiles were lent by Unit Parts "The World of Auto Parts," Doyle Gasoline & Oil Co., William J. Henner and Harper Sibley.

Carriages and wagons came from Mrs. W. Austin Wadsworth of Geneseo, Harper Sibley, the Yates estate through George H. Clune, and James Cunningham and Son Co. An antique piano came from Levis Music Stores, a Civil War flag from Charles Peck, and luggage from Milton Zelter.

The pageant was fascinating as the entire history of Rochester, from its initial settlement to the city of 1934, passed in review from right to left across a huge stage erected in front of the Edgerton Park grandstand. Narrators in niches on each side of the stage talked alternately into microphones as the story evolved.

A prologue opened the program—a forest scene in which the pioneer characters of Mary Jemison, Ebenezer "Indian" Allen, Col. Nathaniel Rochester, Col. William Fitzhugh and Major Charles Carroll appeared. Scene 1 covered the period of 1823 to 1837, in which the infant settlement successively became Rochesterville, then Rochester in 1834. The opening of the Erie Canal in 1825, the arrival of the Tonawanda Railroad in 1834, and the emergence of politician and president-maker Thurlow Weed were shown.

Scene 2 was devoted to the visit of General Washington's Revolutionary War aide, Marquis Lafayette in 1825, as part of his grand tour of the country. The famous leap to death of Sam Patch and his bear at Rochester's upper falls in 1829 was depicted in Scene 3.

Entitled *Staff of Life,* Scene 4 showed the flour-milling of the 1840s, in which industry Rochester was the greatest in the world, thereby acquiring the name of *The Flour City.* Scene 5 depicted *The Young Lion of the West* from 1851 to 1855, in which great names arose in local history: Hiram Sibley, James Vick, John Jacob Bausch, Frederick Douglass and the Fox Sisters.

The Civil War was the subject of Scene 6 as Rochesterians achieved fame on the battlefield: Capt. Henry Lomb, Col. Quimby, Col. Palmer and Capt. Pierce. In Scene 7, entitled *The Four Corners in 1884,* we looked at the 50th year of the city, which boasted such residents as Lewis Swift, Daniel Powers, Nathan Stein, Leopold Bloch, Henry Michaels, Levi Adler, Henry Stein, Susan B. Anthony and George Eastman.

Scene 8, *Trial by Fire,* was devoted to Daniel Powers and his Powers Building, which he determined, by three subsequent additions, to be the tallest in the city, surpassing Daniel Wilder's structure across the street. The Powers Building had the first elevator in the city, and people came downtown to ride "The

Vertical Railway" as it was called then.

George B. Selden, who gained much fame for the city with his horseless carriage experiments and patent litigation, was the subject of Scene 9, dated 1893. The final scene, *Swift Run These Years,* brought the history of the Flower City up to date.

A high point of the Centennial observance was the day Lord Mayor Leech of Rochester, England, visited Edgerton Park to be officially welcomed by his local counterpart, Mayor Stanton. (With all Rochester's "sister cities" in Europe, isn't it strange that Rochester, England, is not one of them?)

A 110–page Centennial book was issued. The price? Twenty-five cents! And printed on slick paper, too. A 10–page souvenier program of the pageant was also available for only 10 cents. The Times-Union daily ran historic pictures on the city, contributed by readers, a feature entitled "Historical Rochester, A Century on Parade." A T-U staff artist ran a one-column feature, "Centenographs," in which historical aspects were noted, accompanied by suitable sketches.

It was a memorable summer in 1934, and those of us who were witness to Rochester's Centennial observance have fond memories of a great event, spectacularly staged, and with exciting history as a background.

TOYS UNDER THE TREE

December 1977

When you were a kid, what kinds of toys did you have? When one passes through a toy store these days, he can't fail to compare the toys of yore with the modern playthings which are meant to keep the kiddies out of mischief.

In our day, practically every boy had a coaster wagon. We remember first having a red and yellow wooden American Hay Wagon. The sides could be removed easily and the vehicle made into a flatbed. As we grew older, we had a red Pioneer All-Steel Wagon. We wore out many pairs of shoes using it almost constantly in the summer. In Rochester, hundreds of kids had an orange-colored coaster wagon, obtainable from Harts' Stores for premium coupons (double coupons on Wednesdays). It was cheap advertising for the grocery chain, and if anyone still has one, it can be considered a collector's item.

For those inclined to build things, there were toys of many kinds. Remember Lincoln Logs? One could make a miniature log cabin, even a frontier settlement from real wooden logs. Or how about Tinker Toy? With wooden sticks and devices to hold them, the possibilities of building structures were many and varied.

But the most famous toy for junior builders was the Erector Set, made by A. C. Gilbert of New Haven, Connecticut. It consisted of metal parts, a screw driver, nuts, bolts, and in the case

Only 2½ years old, but we could drive!

The rocking horse had real hair.

The Buddy-L extention ladder truck was solid steel, good for years of hardy use.

The author enjoys his Christmas Toys.

of larger sets, an electric motor. All this came in a bright red wooden chest. The fault we had with our No. 7 set, which was supposed to build a steam shovel and an elevator, was that the instructions were not precise as to how the motor could be employed in order to operate the gears you assembled in a gear box. We were able to build everything short of the power train.

The Gilbert Company also made chemistry sets, but we never had the urge. One evening, at the home of a cousin, he was working with his set and when he employed a sulphuric compound in one experiment, the resulting stench almost drove everyone from the house! Never saw Uncle Charlie so furious! He really blew his stack on poor Willard that night!

The Moline (Illinois) Pressed Steel Company turned out a great set of toys—Buddy L's, and we had several. You couldn't break them! They were a far cry from the plastic toys of today. The Buddy-L line included such scale models as a pickup truck, steam shovel, concrete mixer (which could make real concrete), sand screener and loader, tow truck, and extension ladder truck. There was another company, Keystone, which produced steel toys such as railroad locomotives and cars on which one could ride.

Practically every boy had an electric train or two. There were several manufacturers engaged in their production: American Flyer, Marx, and Lionel, being the more famous. Lionel's laboratories in New York City came out with new features in the fall of every year. One year it was the "chugger" device for its steam locomotives. Another year, by dropping pellets into a container on the locomotive, smoke would puff from the stack. Then, there were devices to load and unload cars, while another development was automatic couplers, activated when the cars stopped at specific locations in the track layout.

The trains were built of heavy-gauge steel, and the locomotives were especially heavy and impervious to destruction. Before the trend was to smaller-gauge layouts, some even fitting on the top of a card table, the standard-gauge electric train was the big thing, provided you had the floor space to accomodate it.

In the spring, the stores blossomed with a toy one doesn't see much any more, the kite. And for months afterward, the power lines and trees were festooned with the remains of ill-fated kites which became unmanageable for their owners. The brand we remember was the High Flyer Big Ben Tailless Dancing Kite, obtainable for about 25 cents in any pharmacy or toy store. Though a tail wasn't necessary, we always added one for greater stability. After a brief assembly and the addition of a ball of twine, the kite would provide many hours of enjoyment in the brisk wind over vacant lots.

We once built one out of sticks and wrapping paper, a big one about four feet in length, but a sizeable wind was necessary to get it into the air. We recall in the thirties one man who brought a beautiful blue silk kite to a lot on Simpson Road in Irondequoit one Saturday afternoon, and with the aid of a winch on the rear of his car, got it into the air. The line broke and it disappeared to the east.

Once the housing boom after World War II began, open spaces were a premium and kites became fewer in the March skies. Occasionally, one could see a box kite. However, the simplicity of assembly of the tailless kind made it more popular.

Of course, the omnipresent bicycle has always been popular with the young set. Remember when they included such items as a front wire basket, rear stand, siren, rear view mirror, and trouser clamps for the wearer? The present-day bikes have come a long way with their multiple-speed devices, better braking system and speedometers.

In the winter, the big toy was the Flexible Flyer sled. Hundreds of thousands of these were sold. Remember when Maplewood Park Hill near Driving Park Avenue was a mecca for sledding? And before the transformation of Ridge Road West to a speedway, the Flexible Flyers were popular on the hill just south of Maplewood Park Lake.

Toboggans were popular to a lesser degree. Remember when they raced down the slide at Ellison Park? Monroe County Parks Director Bob Cochrane made each rider sign a waiver, releasing the county from responsibility in the event of an accident.

Wind-up toys, iron toys, Teddy bears (named for President Theodore Roosevelt for his unwillingness to kill a bear cub when hunting), stuffed animals, and wooden animals whose moveable parts were connected with rope, all had their places in the affections of the children who possessed them.

Anyone who has any of the above toys in his attic has real collector's items. And there are a number of hobbyists throughout the country who collect rare toys, paying many times the original price to possess them.

The U.S.S. *Akron* at her mast in Akron, Ohio, September 1931. Because of the clean, symmetrical design, she and her sister craft, *Macon* were the two most beautiful rigid dirigibles ever built.

AIRSHIPS OVER WESTERN NEW YORK

March 1978

Next Tuesday will mark the anniversary of the most spectacular air disaster up to April 4, 1933. For on that date, 45 years ago, the U. S. Navy dirigible, *Akron,* dropped into the Atlantic during a storm off Barnegat Light, New Jersey, with a loss of 73 men. There were but three survivors of the shocking tragedy.

Rigid airships have always intrigued us. Since Count Zeppelin's early experiments, these massive ships enjoyed great popularity for about 40 years, though their history was spotted with spectacular accidents. The Rochester area was fortunate to have been visited by some of these craft.

The first to fly over was the 680–foot *Shenandoah,* June 3, 1924. The Navy's first rigid airship, but of obsolete design, was fabricated in Philadelphia, using specifications of the German ship L-49, which was captured in France in World War I. It was our first airship to conduct exercises in mooring to the U.S.S. *Patoka,* the Navy's dirigible mooring vessel. Obsolete or not, the appearance of "Daughter of the Stars" over Rochester, heading toward the setting sun, was a thrilling sight. Amateur radio operators contacted her and were rewarded with a somewhat ungrammatical reply: "You are the first bunch that have woke up today. Best regards."

Radio station WHAM also made contact, and at the request of the *Shenandoah's* skipper, commander Zachary Lansdowne, relayed the ship's position to her home port at Lakehurst, New Jersey. The craft's pioneer radio equipment made communication impossible beyond a 30-mile range.

Fifteen months later the ship, while on a publicity tour of state fairs, broke into three parts in a violent line squall over Caldwell, Ohio, and crashed with a loss of 14, including Commander Lansdowne. Repercussions of the accident were felt in the court-martial trial of General Billy Mitchell, who questioned, "What business has the Navy to be flying over land, anyway?" The Navy defended its policy of letting as many taxpayers as possible see its "battleship of the skies."

On October 15, 1926, the *Los Angeles* sped over the city at 70 mph, enroute from Henry Ford's airport in Detroit to Lakehurst, New Jersey. One newspaper account described the ship as a "giant dragonfly." It was to visit Rochester once again, but at night, and few saw her then. The *Los Angeles* was of advanced design, built for the Navy after World War I. Flown to the United States in 1924 by Dr. Hugo Eckener as payment for German reparations, it became the most successful American airship. Under stipulations of the reparations commission, the ship could not be armed. So it was used for training crews, in experiments in launching and retrieving aircraft, and in exercises in landing on the carrier *Saratoga.* It was dismantled in 1940 after 242 successful flights.

The famous *Graf Zeppelin* almost came to Rochester on the final leg of its round-the-world trip, August 28, 1929. After office employees and factory workers were discharged that afternoon, many trekked to the hills south of the city and maintained an all-night vigil. The Rochester Airport was clogged with visitors. For some unexplained reason, Dr. Eckener, upon leaving Cleveland, struck a course to the southeast, direct to the naval air station at Lakehurst. Times-Union newscaster, Al Sigl, branded the affair as "the night of the great disappointment." However, the writer was one of three recipients in the city who received a letter carried on the 21–day world voyage. Cost was $3.65. Pieces of mail carried from Lakehurst to Lakehurst, via Friederickshafen, Tokyo and Los Angeles totaled 36,000.

The next rigid airship to visit the area was the British *R-100.* Following a flight across the Atlantic to Montreal, the ship hovered over the Ontario Beach area, August 11, 1930. The tuneups for the Canada's Cup yacht races were being held, with the *Thisbe* under William P. Barrows, scheduled to meet the *Quest* a few days later. The *R-100,* floating languidly, could be plainly seen by those who rushed to the tops of downtown office buildings.

Almost two months later, its sister ship, the *R-101,* which had not been given all her tests, was enroute to India with a selected list of passengers, when she slammed into a French hillside near Beuvais and exploded, killing 47. The tragedy ended British experimentation with rigid airships. The *R-100* was dismantled, its duralumin framework pulverized by a steam roller.

The 785–foot U.S.S. *Akron* twice visited Rochester and both were unscheduled events, because of adverse weather which altered its course. On Armistice Day in 1931, the ship's commander, Charles E. Rosendahl, had planned a cruise to Pittsburgh. However, heavy fog caused a route change, which took the craft to the city of its birth, Akron, Ohio. As its homeward course to Lakehurst along the shore of Lake Ontario was followed, Rochesterians were alerted by a news flash from the Times-Union over WHAM. The airport's beacon was turned on early to guide the ship.

The *Akron* turned toward the city at the Genesee River, and in huge circles flew over the downtown area. The writer remembers what looked like a huge silver fish with red, white and green riding lights flashing. When the craft was enroute to the area, Times-Union ace cameraman, Joe Durnherr, raced to the airport, jumped into an open plane piloted by Ray Hylan, and took off to meet the giant. The resulting picture was the first of a moving object taken from a plane in this area. A copy was sent to skipper Rosendahl, who replied with thanks, saying Rochester was one of the most beautifully lighted cities in the country.

The *Akron's* second visit was on the night of January 24, 1933, but very few, other than the Summerville Coast Guards, saw her. Hemmed in by lightning in the east and west, the ship complacently circled about until the disturbance abated, then followed the river to Stutson Street, turned east and vanished into the clouds. Two and a half months later, the wreckage of this magnificent ship was on the bottom of the Atlantic, victim of a violent storm, while engaged in testing radio compass equipment.

When the *Akron's* sister ship, the *Macon,* crashed into the Pacific in February, 1935, the United States gave up experiments with this type of craft. However, in the 1938 naval budget, there was an appropriateion for a three-million-cubic-foot training dirigible. There were squabbles over acceptance of bids, and the project was cancelled, the money diverted to other purposes.

The writer has never wavered from the belief that there is definitely a place in the transportation picture for the rigid airship, but in the commercial field only. With a virtual world monopoly on non-explosive helium as a lifting medium, plus developments in metalurgy, fabric and propulsion which have occurred since the destruction of the *Hindenburg* in 1937, the

United States could become a world leader in rigid airship operation. Size of the craft is limited only by docking facilities.

As airborne cargo carriers, they would be unequaled. As passenger carriers, they would strike a happy medium for those who prefer faster travel than ocean vessels, yet like a slower pace than jet travel. Those who've been aloft in one of these giants say there is nothing to compare with dirigible travel, anywhere. It is an entirely different dimension in long-distance travel.

Elmer R. Messner, one of the most talented of artists in the Rochester area. A gentleman beyond compare, his death was a great loss to his many friends and contemporaries.

FAVORITES IN THE FOURTH ESTATE

July 1978

The Fourth Estate (newspaper business) has been successful because of employees with a wide divergence of talent. However, through movies and television, the average journalist has been stereotyped as a character who smokes endless cigarettes, partakes of the grape frequently, is given to profanity and engaged in any means, fair or foul, to acquire a story. In other words, he assumes the posture of a sort of oddball much of the time. This was generally true years ago. Though there are a handful of them still in newsrooms all over they are also found in any other line of endeavor.

During the writer's 16 years on the staff of the local dailies, he saw countless staffers come and go. A number were unusual in their deportment. But, by and large, we feel that the face of journalism has perceptably changed since World War II. There are things a journalist cannot do any longer, as the laws relating to this business have become more defined; one only has to review the myriad of cases involving newspaper reporting, which have landed in the courts since 1945 as proof.

The period we spent as an adjunct of the Fourth Estate was an education in itself, and we got to know some mighty fine people who have remained our friends. Following, in alphabetical order, are some of those whose friendships we have treasured.

WALLACE BRADLEY, artist. Brad, who had over 50 years of service before his retirement, has long been interested in theatre history, silent movies, rail transportation and baseball. It was an almost daily ritual during a break in routine to amble out to Brad's corner and have a go at something nostalgic. A nice, amiable fellow.

CLAUDE BROWN, photographer. Whenever we had something of a photographic nature to do, Brownie was more than ready to accomodate us. Long a Times-Union shutter bug, he was particularly adept with animals and small children. He has a rare gift to make one laugh, anytime.

CLIFFORD E. CARPENTER, Chief editorial writer. Cliff, one of the first-class gentlemen in the business, reminds us of the brilliant Eric Sevareid. Soft spoken, well-educated, read and traveled, he is the type from whom one could always learn something when in his presence. A real tower (he is about 6'6" tall) in his writing profession—he has done it all.

BOB CARTER, artist. Since major league baseball is of great interest to us, becoming friends with Bob was inevitable as he saw some of the early Hall of Famers in action. His favorite was the immortal Walter Johnson, the modest pitcher whose fast ball was unequaled in his time. The stories Bob told of these athletes were many.

HENRY W. CLUNE, columnist. One could write a book on this beautiful man whose style of writing is in a class by itself. He can describe a miniscule chimney fire in his Scottsville home with so much vividness that the reader can smell the soot and hear the clang of fire apparatus. Though he has rubbed shoulders with the greats in the arts and professions, Mr. Clune remains a modest man, as always. Loves English bull terriers, of which he had several, and his wife, Charlotte Boyle Clune, a former all-star swimming champ. (I assume Henry likes them in reverse order!)

DON GREENLEA, Calendar of Events editor. Here is a young man who possesses a most friendly personality and a hearty chuckle. A meticulous worker, he has been on top of his job for many years. It was always a pleasure to spend a few minutes with Don, as he was good medicine when we were experiencing a bad day.

ESTELLE HEICKLEN, picture librarian. Of all the persons who worked in the reference library from 1956–1972, Estelle was the most congenial, and it was a sad day when she moved to California. Personality personified, she was ideal to hold the position, her friendly smile always a decided asset.

HOWARD C. HOSMER, Assistant Managing Editor. We have known Howard since 1947, when he was instructor of a journalism course at RBI. He has always been willing to pass on helpful suggestions, and was prone to write notes of praise whenever a worthy project was completed. A terrific writer, too, his "It's This Way" was a much-read colomn for years, and his year-end mention of the area's noted personalities served as a Who's Who of Monroe County.

ELMER R. MESSNER, Editorial Cartoonist. Now we speak of one of the true greats in the business. When it comes to artistry in his chosen profession, plus his gentlemanly characteristics, Mr. Messner, as we always respectfully addressed him, is in a class by himself. The mold was junked when he was born. Winner of innumerable awards, locally and nationally, he for years has been a leading light in two national cartoonists' associations. He has great talent as a painter of landscapes, too. Possessor of a most even-tempered demeanor, one can't help like this man when in his company but five minutes. We did, even before becoming a colleague at the paragraph factory.

BEULAH PASCH, Secretary to the Democrat & Chronicle Managing Editor. In the days of libbers, zany attire, free lifestyle, and whatever, it was a revelation to see a real lady perform her duties in a steady, efficient and proper manner. Miss Pasch served 11 managing editors and one learned of the high esteem in which each held her when she was given a party upon retirement. A column, attesting to her value, appeared in the paper under Cliff Carpenter's by-line. They don't make many like Beulah Pasch these days, if at all!

PAUL PINCKNEY, Sports Editor. It was always a pleasure to talk with his knowledgeable man. Many sports pundits are breezy, arrogant, and overly impressed by their supposed importance, but not Paul. He had an inner gift which would lend itself, whether he were interviewing an athlete or merely talking with a colleague. A very fine fellow, Paul.

ROGER J. REYNOLDS, Chief copy boy. Due to our mutual interest in silent movies, we hit it off well together. He's a walking encyclopedia on the subject and could pick up some loose change were he to engage in lecturing before clubs, church groups, etc. Now a bank officer, Roger is still the same affable guy we first met over 20 years ago.

PAUL A. ROBERTSON, Composing Room. A friendly, affable fellow with whom it was a pleasure to ride home after work. Knowledgeable in many areas, this long-distance-runner and Massachusetts native has continued to keep in touch after retiring from the paragraph factory. He and his charming wife, Doris, make the ideal couple.

CLIFFORD SMITH, General Assignment Reporter. Cliff can be easily identified by a rolling gait, probably acquired during destroyer service off Korea; a ready smile and chuckle; and a militant defense of Ted Williams over Joe DiMaggio. A clean-cut young man from Braintree, Massachusetts, he possesses fine habits which any father would be pleased to see his son emulate. An authority on musicians of the Great Band Era, Cliff has an extensive record collection, dating back to that period. He's interviewed some of the musical greats: Buddy Rich, Jimmy & Marian McPartland, Carl Dengler, etc., but was rebuffed by Rosemary Clooney because she was "too tired" the morning after her concert here. A swell fellow and a very good friend, Cliff Smith.

DESMOND STONE, Editorial Writer. New Zealand-born, Des really knows how to treat the Queen's English. English grammar, if written and spoken properly, is a very beautiful language, and Des is a leading exponent of that belief. Looking over his shoulder one day in the newsroom, we discovered his method for writing. His procedure is to write his initial draft in long-hand, revise a couple times, then type the final copy. We have used this method ever since. Small wonder that his "Winds of Change" series in the Times-Union won several awards. A fine gentleman and a credit to the writing profession.

PETER S. STUTZ, City Deskman. Another of our good friends who was always willing to discuss baseball. Peter was usually the first man to arrive at the D&C city desk, so that was quite convenient for our periodic discussions. Great guy.

BOB WHITE, Sportswriter. Before he left Gannett for a greener city room, Bob was a walking encyclopedia of baseball trivia, and his constant questions along these lines enriched our storehouse of knowledge. One guy we hated to see leave town.

We trust that the foregoing has served to dispel any ideas that the journalism profession is overloaded with kooks and characters. There are some, make no mistake about that. But, at least in the time we served Gannett, there were some very fine people there. The foregoing are those whom we remember and respect most.

CARL DENGLER
DEAN OF BANDSMEN

October 1978

Through the years, it has been our good fortune to become acquainted with some very wonderful people from many walks of life. One of these whom we place in the top rank is Carl J. Dengler, Rochester's veteran orchestra leader.

We have known Carl a number of years, our friendship beginning via the telephone. Seeing reference to him in the daily papers, we communicated with him and in no time at all, Carl was enriching our knowledge of musicians and other show business folk, for he is gifted with an astounding memory of those with whom he has come in contact, as well as events which have occurred during the past 55 years or so.

He was brought up on the city's west side in a neighborhood whose people prided themselves in keeping up their property. His father, Jacob Dengler, was a merchant tailor and custom designer, having a shop on West Main Street, capable of turning out 130 suits a week. Custom tailors are the elite of the clothing business, and the senior Dengler was rewarded with assignments from show business personalities, sports figures, politicians, judges, etc. He even serviced prominent persons from out of town who sent their measurements to him by mail.

Carl remembers some of these personages: Singer's Midgets,

Carl Dengler puts in some practice time in his studio. The walls are graced with autographed pictures of friends and associates. When in town, many consider it a "must" to visit Carl.

Bert Lahr, Joe Penner, "Sliding" Billy Watson, "Bozo" Snyder (one of the funniest men in show business), playwright George Brooks and producer George Abbott. Thus, show business was infused into Carl's veins at an early age.

At 12, Carl was told the shocking news that he had night blindness (retinitis) which would cause him eventual loss of sight. "Realizing the problem I was facing for the rest of my life, I started to form plans for ways of coping with situations with which I'd be confronted. Basically, I began to develop a visual memory bank during the remaining time I had vision. It has been proven invaluable in later life, when others have forgotten cherished memories."

At the age of seven, however, Carl had begun his first drum lessons with Frank Brownell, and marimba lessons with Frank's daughter, Laura, who was the drummer of Pearl Dodge's "Harmony Girls" orchestra. At 10, he began studying modern dance drumming with Floyd "Tommy" Thomas, one of the greats of the day.

He made his public debut at 14, playing with the Madison Junior High School dance orchestra (which he helped organize) on WHEC's "Buster Brown" program. The band played once a week for a year and a half, and Carl got the munificient sum of $2 for each 15-minute show. This was about 1929.

Later, he played for well-known band leaders Art Taylor, Sax Smith, Johnny Schwab and Hughie Barrett. Came 1935, Carl organized his "Rainbow Rhythm Orchestra," and it has been going strong ever since. His theme song, "I'm Always Chasing Rainbows," is most appropriate, for in his words, "I try to make musical portraits in color. I always was fascinated with the beauty of rainbows."

In the late thirties, he played sweet and swing music for country clubs and colleges for three years, and had a 32-week engagement at the old Hotel Seneca, beginning on June 4, 1938. Then came a year on the *SS Argentine,* playing from New York to Buenos Aires, with ports of call in between, where Carl enhanced his knowledge of Latin-American rhythms. This was followed by a seven-year, six-night-a-week stand at the unforgettable Odenbach Peacock Room at Main & Clinton, closing on April 7, 1947.

Few musicians have established a chronological history of their engagements through the years, but Carl has. It was a fascinating experience for this writer to thumb through the pages of his scrapbooks, filled with pictures, programs, announcements, and dated clippings which chronicle the musical life of Carl Dengler. What a background for a book!

His philosophy on aspects of the music business gets right to the root of things. About the decline of the bands, he mentions several reasons:

"The swing era took over with such great musicians as Tommy Dorsey, Benny Goodman, Artie Show and Charlie Barnet. When side men became featured and the arrangers wrote for them, they began to lose the communication with the dancing crowds.

"Then the government delivered a knockout blow to hotel and nightclub dancing by imposing a 30% dancing-and-entertainment tax during World War II. That was legalized political larceny, based on greed and stupidity. It broke the back of the hotel business and killed off the clean operators. And instead of repealing it as the politicians promised, they merely reduced it to 20%. After the damage was done by destroying the one good proving ground of many young, talented entertainers, the tax was finally repealed.

"Other causes of the big bands' decline were World War II and the draft, which broke up many of the great organizations, and after the conflict, the steadily rising costs of doing business, which made it virtually impossible to continue tours of one-night stands for most aggregations."

Carl also has thoughts on what is called "music" today. "There are too many performers making too much money with little or no talent. The screamers who are classed as singers, and the ones who play to ruin one's ears, just leave me cold. I like a nice beat, a good melody line, played by competent musicians who can read music and improvise in good musical taste. And I like musicians who make a good, clean appearance."

For the past 25 years or so, Carl's orchestra has been featured in many of the prominent social events in New York and northern Pennsylvania. He has appeared on radio and television, both as a performer and talk-show guest. Recently, he appeared on CBL, Toronto, from coast to coast, on a talk-and-record show known as *Fresh Air,* hosted by Bill McNeil and Cy Strange.

He is also a teacher of percussion instruments and piano and is a vocal coach. And if that weren't enough, as a composer he has written some works which have been performed in concert by his orchestra and others. The Maestro is doing research on a book which will cover activities of many persons with whom he has come in contact during his 63 years. Carl has crossed paths with famous musicians and entertainers: Freddy Martin, Bobby Hackett, Phil Napoleon, Joe Venuti, Vincent Lopez, Frankie Carl, Roger Williams, Tommy Dorsey, and Guy Lombardo. Since his forte is playing percussion instruments, Gene Krupa, Buddy Rich, Louis Bellson, Ray McKiney, John Back, Don LaMonde, Dave Tough, Morey Feld and George Wettling have been friends, also.

The stories he has told about these people would make fascinating reading if put into a book. Carl has been privy to material on the personal lives of many, and though it would be of interest to the sensation seekers, this will not get into his book. Carl is not a purveyor of the offbeat.

He has been happily married to his wife, Ginny, for 38 years. "She has been steering the Dengler ship of state all this time through the many vicissitudes of life. To her, I am deeply indebted for her faithfulness, support, cheerful personality and golden smile."

For this writer, a mere telephone conversation with Rochester's premier orchestra leader is an educational experience. A person is never too old to learn, especially at the hands of a teacher of the competence of Carl J. Dengler. May he enjoy many years of good health, happiness, and fine music.

SNOW-FIGHTING 50 YEARS AGO

November 1978

With the approach of winter's chill winds, municipal personnel busily engage in preparing snow-fighting equipment for the onslaught of the elements. In the thirties, the City of Rochester had one of the finest systems to cope with big snowfalls of any city of comparable size in the country.

The "generalissimo" of this snow-fighting army was balding, good-natured Edwin A. Miller, superintendent of maintenance of the Department of Public Works. In the summer, he oversaw road construction and cleaning and refuse removal, but as the autumn leaves started to fall, Miller turned more of his attention to the winter ahead. Plow mechanisms were affixed to trucks, spreaders attached to the rear of sand trucks, and other details attended to so that with the first storm's approach, all units were in readiness for the zero-hour attack.

The superintendent's office was in the Dewey Avenue garage. He maintained constant communication with the U.S. Weather Bureau in the old Federal Building (now the "new" City Hall). The meteorologist was Jesse L. Vanderpool, in case you have forgotten. Everyone knew who he was during the 59 consecutive hours of sub-zero temperatures in February, 1934, when the mercury hit the record low of 22 below zero, and in

July, 1936, when the mercury climbed to a record 102. Vanderpool's office eventually was relocated at the old Rochester Airport on Scottsville Road when aviation grew in importance.

When Miller received word that a storm was approaching, he alerted the area sidewalk and road supervisors, who in turn notified plow crews to stand by. When the snow achieved a depth of a few inches, the city's 100 to 125 horse-drawn sidewalk plows were ordered out. Each was pulled by two stalwart draft horses, and the faithful animals plodded through the worst weather, bells on their harnesses jingling in the crisp air. Each driver achieved the appearace of the abominable snowman. There were no cabs or windshields to offer protection. Yet, men and beasts did a grand job—even better in some respects than what is accomplished today.

If the storm continued, 50 to 75 roadway plows were then ordered out. City-owned trucks handled the work in the central traffic district, while privately-contracted vehicles worked the remaining districts. We recall one truck used for years in the streets of the 17th Ward, whch borders Irondequoit. It was a huge, green, chain-driven, hard-rubber-tired bulldog Mack and no drift was too much for it. It always bullied its way through!

Once the storm let up, the mopping-up process began. Crews of shovelers were dispatched to churches, where weddings and funerals were scheduled, to clear away the snow in front. Other crews with ash wagons or trucks were used downtown to clear the crosswalks. Pay in the thirties was around 40 cents an hour. At night six snow loaders continuously fed the white stuff into dump trucks, which deposited their loads into the river through chutes in the Broad or Bausch bridges.

Sand was used initially to aid traction, but after discovering it clogged the storm drains, cinders were used as the medium.

Rochester had 100 to 125 of these horse-drawn sidewalk plows before motorized equipment replaced them.

When they were found to be too messy, a cinder-salt mixture was selected, and finally, this was replaced by an all-salt weapon against ice. Area automobiles would never be the same again.

Aiding the Department of Public Works in the thirties was the New York State Railways. Ever since the first horse car trundled up Exchange Street in 1862, it was mandatory for the street railway, by terms of its franchise, to keep the area of the street used by its rolling stock clear of snow. Thus, the trolley company employed a dozen sweepers, seven or eight plows and several sand cars for this purpose. How many Irondequoiters remember this equipment being used on the Summerville, Sea Breeze and Sodus Bay lines? With the ending of trolley service in 1941, the obligation of the transit company was removed.

Edwin A. Miller ran a highly efficient army of snow fighters, but he met his Waterloo in December, 1944. A snowstorm of gigantic proportions hit the city with such dire consequences that no vehicular traffic moved for days. Buses and cars were abandoned where they stalled in the drifts—even downtown. Only the subway was operating, and on time. Rochester, which had long been called "the best-governed city," had to swallow its pride and accept the offer of Governor Dewey of state plows.

Of course, there was the inevitable investigation as to why the city was "caught with its plows up." After the political charges and countercharges, someone had to go; someone had to be the sacrificial lamb, albeit the scapegoat. Ed Miller was fired after so many years of faithful service.

However, even if the most efficient man had held the position, the result in 1944 would have been exactly the same. The snowfall was just too much to cope with. Witness Oswego some years later when Rochester furnished plows to that beleagured city. One has only to remember the great storms of the winter of 1977–78 to recall the chaos all over the country.

As long as methods of battling winter storms in the old days are discussed, however, the name of Edwin A. Miller will always be remembered as an efficient general-in-chief of Rochester's army of snowfighters.

Earl F. White, elementary algebra teacher at old Irondequoit High. He believed in hard work, but was respected by his students.

MEMORIES OF HIGH SCHOOL TEACHERS

September 1979

How many of you remember your high school teachers? The ones from whom we received our education were at old Irondequoit High School, that ancient pile of red brick, located at the corner of Titus Avenue and Cooper Road. Let us return to those days of the thirties and forties and reawaken memories. We have some excellent ones.

CLAYTON W. CARROLL, Civics and Economic Citizenship, Room 26. He was our first instructor upon entering the school in 1937, and our class was his first, having been graduated from teachers college a few months previously. He was a fine instructor, very personable with a hearty laugh, but could readily establish discipline if the need arose. Lives in retirement in Florida and does considerable traveling.

EARL F. WHITE, Elementary Algebra, Room 30. A short, stocky man, he had the handshake of a vise. And how he could demonstrate at the blackboard! "You factor X to the fourth, minus Y to the fourth into X to the second, minus Y to the second—Klos, you got it?" We rarely did, but somehow Mr. White got us through the course. He was violently opposed to the students' writing on their desks, and he daily applied an eraser to markings. Died in 1978.

MARY R. MEDDEN, English I, Room 28. A short, attractive teacher, she had the habit of sitting atop her desk, crossing her legs, and inspiring her students in discussions of Scott's *Ivanhoe,* Coleridge's *Rhyme of the Ancient Mariner,* Shakespeare's *Julius Caesar* and Hough's *Covered Wagon.* A stickler for good grammar, she became completely unglued one day upon asking a student why he wasn't writing for a test. He replied, "I ain't got no pencil." It sure was in the fan for a few minutes afterward! In light of the present slaughter of the beautiful English language, Miss Medden, where are you now"? Deceased.

WARREN P. PIERSON, General Science, Room 25. "Pop", as he was affectionately known, knew his subject very well, but his long dissertations on the "factors of our environment" or the "evils of alcohol" sometimes made us sleepy by the end of the fifth period. It affected him, too, as his voice would play tricks, its pitch occasionally rising. This was alleviated by gulping cough drops. Deceased.

MARGARET CROSLEY, English II, Room 34. She had an elusive air about her, a shell which was hard to understand. A most capable teacher, but for some mysterious reason, she allowed only two and a half hours for the final exam. All others were of three-hour duration. Didn't have time to review our answers, but we passed. Living in Ohio.

RICHARD C. TEFFT, Plane Geometry, Room 36. A very likeable fellow who later became assistant principal of the school, "Dick" loved the kids and loathed cracking down on fun-makers. No wonder we had to take special instruction Wednesdays after school! Mr. Tefft was principal of Balston Spa High School when he died a few years ago.

WILLIAM "RED" MAMMOSSER, Accounting and Business Law, Room 38. Though we had no classes with him, his was our homeroom while a sophomore. And boy, did he hate whistling and shirts hanging outside trousers! No matter where you were, you didn't whistle within range of him or you'd hear the yell, "Cut out the whistling!" Never found out if he liked Elmo Tanner's whistling version of *Heartaches* with Ted Weems' band. This brush-cut Syracuse grad, who coached the IHS football team for a time, is retired and still living in Irondequoit.

CAROLYN TITUS SIMMONS, European and American History, Room 16. A teacher of very short physical stature, she more than compensated for this by her unquestioned knowledge of her subjects. As a means of constant review, she asked question after question. We'd occasionally arouse her displeasure by having the answer before she finished asking. "Lloyd, would you please let someone else answer once in awhile?," she'd plead with a wry smile. Her classes were the ones we enjoyed to the exclusion of all others. This was proved by our final grades, our best in high school: 97 for American History, 90 for modern European history. Died in 1960.

EVERETT R. THOMAS, Typing. Long intrigued by the typewriter, we seized the opportunity to learn to operate this machine. Mr. Thomas, who rarely smiled, was an excellent instructor, and to encourage perfect copies, instituted a contest which involved "traveling" from New York to Chicago. Every perfect copy earned for the student advancement to the next station. It may sound corny, but Mr. Thomas turned out some excellent typists as a result. As a writer, we owe our typing prowess to him.

JANETTE B. WILSON, English III, Room 20. A tall, very attractive brunette with a good sense of humor, Miss Wilson's classes were marked by the study of novels such as Rolvaag's *Giants in the Earth,* Lewis's *Arrowsmith,* and Tarkington's *The*

Turmoil. One of the hardest working teachers in the school, she also taught a couple classes in Journalism, and was advisor to the school paper, *The Rodequoit,* which kept her busy, often after 5 p.m. An instructor who addressed her students with "Mr." or "Miss," she is living in Snyder, New York.

HELEN L. REGENSBURGER, Advanced Mathematics, Room 31. She apparently believed that procrastination is the thief of time, because even during study periods, she made sure every student was doing something. "Donald, get busy," she would implore. And if anyone kicked up in class, someone was bound to pipe up, "Throw him out, Miss Reg." She was highly respected, however, and the senor annual *Neodaondaquat* (Indian name, one of 50 for Irondequoit) in 1941 was dedicated to her. Still lives in Irondequoit.

MARTHA A. LITTLER, Public Speaking, Dramatics & Debate. Always liking to speak before an audience, we seized the opportunity while a senior to take a year of Public Speaking. Miss Littler hailed from the Boston area, which was more than proved by her heavy New England accent. She looked a bit like Gloria Swanson. We enjoyed PS so much that we always volunteered to be the first to speak. In the second half of the 1940–41 school year, we induced five others to sign up for Debate, thereby realizing more opportunities to think fast on one's feet. Miss Littler ably directed the senior play, *And Let Who Will Be Clever,* and the National Honor Society's production, *One Mad Night.* Lives in South Fallsburg, New York, where she is active in the Forestburgh Playhouse.

HARRY A. WAGNER, German, Economics, Room 32. Here was a likeable teacher who promised his students at the start of the year, "If you play ball with me, I'll play ball with you." Discipline problems were nonexistent in his classes, and the students had a warm, friendly feeling for this excellent teacher.

One of his two sons is a musician and this aspect was hereditary. Mr. Wagner's father was Victor Wagner, who led the Eastman Theatre Orchestra for many years. It was a genuine loss for the school when Mr. Wagner retired a few years back. Former students still identify with him wherever they are—in this country or abroad. (Lived in Irondequoit until his death in 1986.)

IRENE H. PRATT, English IV, Room 33. Here was a no-nonsense instructor who excelled in teaching the fine art of English composition, especially business letters. As a writer, we are greatly indebted to her for what we learned under her guidance. One of the best! She drove a sporty blue Hudson convertible to school. Lived in Trinidad until her death in 1979.

HELEN F. RICE, Librarian. Every day, if possible, we'd spend a period in the library, which was housed in one of the old portables. Daily newspapers, magazines and reference works were the drawing cards, and personable Miss Rice helped us take advantage of them. She always assigned us to Table A, Seat 1, which was close to the magazine rack and reference section. Perfect for a fellow destined to be a researcher and writer! And so quiet, even to the noiseless Remington typewriter. Miss Rice, retired and an avid bird lover, still lives in Irondequoit.

ALFRED C. HAMILTON, Principal. He was a stern taskmaster, but during his administration, discipline problems were minimal. Being sent to the principal's office was a thing to be avoided! Because of his gruff exterior, the pranksters did not like him, naturally. But we got along very well with him from the time we entered school in September, 1937, until he presented us our diploma in June, 1941. Mr. Hamilton also served as superintendent of Dictrict 3, which included two grammar schools then, Reuben A. Dake and Hosea Rogers. Deceased.

What wonderful four years of memories of the fine teachers we have! And it all seems yesterday, even after three wars, the vicissitudes of economics and eight U. S. presidents. Tempus fugit!

OLD 999

April 1980

Steam railroad enthusiasts, and there are thousands in the United States, derive feelings of nostalgia when the famous 999 locomotive, which once pulled the Empire State Express, is mentioned.

The historic engine and tender are now on permanent display at the Chicago Museum of Science & Industry. When there in 1977, we had the pleasure of seeing the grand old gal of the rails and were gratified that the unit has been saved. Railroad history was made by 999 in upstate New York in May, 1893.

Prior to 1890, the New York Central and Hudson River Railroad, the line of Commodore Vanderbilt, had enjoyed a steady rise in its passenger traffic. Faster trains were added as business dictated, but none achieved the popularity and prestige as the Empire State Express, which began service in the autumn of 1891.

In the general passenger agent's office of the Central was a genius for railroad publicity, George H. Daniels. One of his achievements was the publishing, in booklet form, Elbert Hubbard's inspiring *Message to Garcia,* for distribution to the employees. Daniels also created and edited a house organ, *The Four-Track News.*

When the new Empire State Express was about to be placed in service, Daniels gave it much publicity. A trial run from New

York to Buffalo was made in September, 1891, carrying a large group of newspapermen among the passengers. The 436–mile trip was made in seven hours and six minutes, at an average speed of 61.40 mph. This was a notable achievement, and the newsmen spread the word in advance of the train's first scheduled westbound trip the following month.

For nearly a year, the train operated westbound only, but it was a great success. It consisted of a combination cafe-coach, two day coaches, and a parlor car. To maintain its swift running time, a dining car was not included. A kitchen was installed in the cafe-coach, and meals were served in the coaches on small tables.

Eventually, an eastbound trip was inaugurated, the train leaving Buffalo at 1 p.m., Rochester at 2:54, Syracuse at 4:00, Albany at 7:00, and reaching New York a little after 10 p.m.

With the Chicago World's Fair scheduled in 1893, the railroads made special preparations to handle the crowds and faster locomotives were built. The New York Central turned to William Buchanan, its superintendent of motive power, to design what became the fastest locomotive in the world. After his stint at the drafting boards, the road's shops in West Albany built the most beautiful engine ever seen in America up to that time.

"Greyhound" best described the unit, numbered 999. She had 84–inch driving wheels, and when the throttle was advanced in her tests, she fairly shot ahead. In the spring of 1893, the engine was thoroughly tested on the well-ballasted roadbed, then was hitched to the Empire to begin regular service from Syracuse to Buffalo.

Came the historic day, May 10, 1893. The train was poised at the old Syracuse station, steam up, for its 150-mile run to Buffalo. The engineer, Charles F. Hogan, was told that in light of the perfect weather to "take the bridle off 999." The platform was crowded with excited onlookers as word had gone out that a new

Once the world's fastest locomotive, old 999 is shown in its original form in Syracuse. With smaller wheels and pilot, it is now at the Chicago Museum of Science & Industry.

world record was to be attempted.

The train adhered to its schedule to Rochester. From here to Batavia, up over Bergen Hill, it continued and on a slightly rising grade for two miles west of Batavia. Then on 14 miles of perfectly level track, Hogan notched the throttle wide open! The officials back in the coaches caught their breath; they had been told to expect fast time that day. When some of them held stopwatches before their eyes, they were astonished. Fast time, indeed! This was incredible!

Several watches confirmed that one of those miles was covered at 112.5 mph. Other miles were run in 38, 41 and 42 seconds respectively. A new world's record for travel had been made. Legend has it that engineer Hogan's hair changed from deep brown to snowy white as the result of his record-setting trip.

The record stood until June 12, 1905, when a high-wheeled locomotive, pulling the Pennsylvania Special near Ada, Ohio, established a new record of 127.06 mph.

The 999 was immediately withdrawn from service and sent to Chicago, where it became a major feature of the World's Fair. Afterwards, it, heading the Empire; the Central's historic *DeWitt Clinton;* and the locomotive *Empress,* pulling an English train, all toured eastern cities.

After the tour, 999 again headed the Empire in regular service. A few years later,she was withdrawn from mainline duty. The locomotive was designed for great speed, not pulling power. Increasing passenger traffic, much of it overnight, demanded larger, heavier trains, complete with pullmans, diners, baggage-express cars, railway post offices and observation cars.

The 84-inch drivers on 999 were replaced by smaller wheels and pilot. For a time she was all but forgotten, hauling an ignominious milk train from Watertown to Carthage. Practically from the scrap heap she was saved by concerned Central officers. Though she was refurbished and given her old number, the 84-inch drivers and original pilot were not reinstalled.

The engine and tender became objects of nostalgia at public historical displays. For a weekend after World War II, the unit was shown at the Atlantic Avenue yards of the Central in Rochester. In the sixties, it was pulled—backwards, mind you—by a diesel unit to Chicago, where it was placed on permanent display.

We were a bit apprehensive when we saw it. It stands on a short stretch of track outside, taking what the elements have to offer. The cab, made of wood, is not liable to survive the rigors of rain, snow, sleet and hot sun forever. The place for such a distinguished object is inside the museum. We remember that every one of the hundreds of Berkshire, Mohawk, Hudson and Niagara locomotives was scrapped during the regime of Robert R. Young and Alfred Perlman in the fifties. Only the *DeWitt Clinton* of 1831 vintage, now in the Ford Museum in Dearborn, Michigan, and the 999 unit remain. Preserving these remnants of steam power from this famous railroad should be paramount.

Lowell Thomas—world traveler, writer, news commentator, lecturer, skiier and friend of the famous wherever he went.

INDESTRUCTABLE LOWELL THOMAS

August 1980

"Good evening, everybody!"

Those words, spoken in a resonant, strident voice, were heard by radio listeners for half a century, and once a person heard that salutation, he never forgot it. He was hearing the man who had traveled more miles than anyone on earth, been to every continent and country, hob-nobbed with the great and near-great, and in general, has seen considerable history made firsthand for over 80 years as no one has seen it. The man, of course, is Lowell Thomas.

Early life was exciting for the future world traveler, writer and radio news reporter, who was born in Woodington, Ohio, April 6, 1892. Nearby lived the famed markswoman, Annie Oakley. When his father finished his doctor's training, the Thomas family moved to Cripple Creek, Colorado, a rough mining town with all sorts of characters. Young Lowell never cared much for Sunday School until he laid eyes on the attractive teacher who taught in the area.

She was none other than Mary Louise Cecile Guinan, later known as "Texas," a brassy blonde, who became famous in the twenties as the Queen of the Speakeasies in New York. Her "Hello, sucker," and "Give the little girl a great big hand," accompanied by the sounds of noisy kleeter-clappers, became her trademarks during the Roaring Twenties in Gotham.

Lowell's father was the molding force in his life. He taught his son the value of reading good books, and the future traveler became a voracious reader of history, geography and biography. Also, the father taught him the priceless art of public speaking by taking him out to the woods and giving him lessons on voice range, inflection, diction, and audience psychology. It was to serve him in good stead through his busy life.

Lowell had assorted jobs in his youth. In the sixth grade he delivered papers, arising at three in the morning. His route took him through the red-light district which every mining town had. He worked as a cattle rancher, a miner, and as a writer on several newspapers, which gave him training for his career. Not neglecting his education, he had three college degrees by the time he was 20.

While teaching at Princeton when the United States entered World War I, he was recommended to President Wilson, who had also taught at Princeton, as the man to collect information on the conflict for the people back home. Traveling was down Lowell's alley, as he had previously visited the Yukon and Alaska.

The U. S. government could not fund the trip, so he went, hat in hand, to some wealthy meat packers and industrialists in Chicago whom he once befriended, and in no time at all he had $100,000 pledged from 18 millionaires. Before he left for Europe, he married a girl he had known in his college days, promising her a world war for their honeymoon.

Visiting France and Italy, he had the good fortune one day, upon returning from the Italian front, to see on an impromptu bulletin board a dispatch announcing the appointment of General Edmund Allenby as commander of British forces in the Middle East. Thomas, recalling this leader's brilliant record in the Boer

War and elsewhere, reasoned that something big was in the wind with the new assignment.

He literally burned wires for permission to go to the area and shortly was cleared. It became the turning point of his life. For not only was Lowell Thomas witness to Allenby's campaign to capture Jerusalem (taking his initial airplane trips in the process), he accompanied a brilliant young British officer, Lt. Thomas E. Lawrence, the famed "Lawrence of Arabia."

Lawrence was the adhesive, the inspiring leader, who bound the varied Arab factions together to drive out the Turks, thereby breaking up the centuries-old Ottoman Empire. By hitting hard, fast, and often, Lawrence's bands overturned many Turkish trains, ruptured supply lines, and severed communications. Lowell Thomas was eyewitness to all this, and his ample notes taken daily served as background material for his best-selling *With Lawrence In Arabia,* written after the war, and which went into more than 100 printings. It was read the world over.

When the Armistice came in November, 1918, Thomas was in France, then went to post-war Germany to cover the precarious political and economic situations there. He returned to America and edited 100,000 feet of movie film, exposed during his wartime assignments. Dramatic scenes, narrated by Thomas, interspersed with musical background, was the format. His presentation, initially shown in New York's Century Theatre, broke all attendance records. The show was taken to London, where it was a smash for another 12 weeks.

Lowell Thomas, now thoroughly accepted as a world traveler and lecturer, was constantly on the go, showing films, and writing as well. Another of his milestones was his interviewing the German sea raider of World War I, Count Felix Von Luckner (who later appeared several times in Rochester to lecture), which resulted in another best-selling book in 1925,

Count Luckner, the Sea Devil. Luckner was a flamboyant, muscular, six-foot-three character, but greatly respected by friend and foe alike. Because of humanitarian beliefs, not a single enemy lost his life when confronted by Luckner on his raiding ship, *Sea-Adler.*

In 1930, CBS was looking for a replacement for the flamboyant, hard-drinking, renowned newscaster, Floyd Gibbons. After a number had auditioned, CBS boss, William S. Paley, and other network brass selected Lowell Thomas after a 15-minute audition. On September 29, 1930, the ubiquitous world traveler went on the air for the first of over 7,800 nightly newscasts. The spot was 15 minutes before "Amos 'n Andy," so in retrospect the back-to-back programming helped both shows, audience-wise.

His broadcasts were done in studios throughout the country, because no mere radio program served as a deterrent to Lowell Thomas in his quest for adventure. He also served as the voice of Fox Movietone News, the weekly feature shown in hundreds of theatres.

In the spring of 1935 he visited Rochester and was escorted around town by Bausch & Lomb executive, Carl S. Hallauer. They posed appropriately near the B&L plant at a street sign, "Lowell Street." They should have proceeded northward and posed in Irondequoit at a similar sign proclaiming "Thomas Avenue."

While in the city, the famed interviewer became interviewee. He stated to reporters that his work was never tiresome. "With the Lindbergh trial ended, the Johnson-Coughlin-Long radio scrap moves to the front in importance," he averred. This was in reference to the philosophies of NRA administrator Hugh S. Johnson; the Detroit radio priest, Father Coughlin of the National Union for Social Justice; and Louisiana "Kingfish," Senator Huey Long. All expounded their economic theories in the press and over radio.

Thomas exhibited a keen appreciation of the value of humor on his broadcasts. As a means of keeping the news from becoming too heavy, he was a leading light in the Tall Story Club, often regaling his listeners with a story told him by one of the members. He was a publicist for the House of David, a baseball team whose bearded members played the game for the fun of it. The Explorer's Club, composed of leading travelers of the world, was also given publicity by their fellow member.

Once in a very great while, Lowell lost his composure during a newscast and got to laughing heartily over an amusing anecdote. So rare was this that the occasions have been recorded by Kermit Schafer's "Pardon My Blooper."

In 1949, Thomas, with son Lowell, Jr. and a small party, set off for Tibet as the first Americans to receive permission to enter that country and its "forbidden capital," Lhasa. They had an audience with the Dalai Lama, the boy ruler, and were allowed to take pictures by special permission. But on the return from this successful venture, a balky horse threw Thomas, breaking his hip in eight places. Largely through the resourcefulness of his son, who had a makeshift litter erected and organized the carrying party, the world's premier traveler was brought back to civilization after an agonizing three weeks of jostling on the rocky trails enroute. The episode was shown at the Eastman Theatre as part of an illustrated program, narrated by Lowell, Jr.

In the fifties, Thomas was a promoter and backer of the wide-screen movie process "Cinerama," a revolutionary method of projection. It was our pleasure to view every Cinerama production when it appeared at Rochester's Monroe Theatre and, to our way of thinking, nothing has equaled it since.

When television came along, Lowell was right in step with his "High Adventure" series, which showed places he visited all over the globe. A geography book brought to life! He also narrated a series of half-hour historical documentaries, each covering a year from 1920 through 1960, and utilizing priceless newsreel film, long stored in vaults.

With his famous voice known throughout the world, plus his writing of over 50 books, he has rubbed shoulders with many famous people. A list of these personages is a veritable "Who's Who of the World." When asked which person impressed him as being the most intelligent, the immediate reply was "Herbert Hoover." The ex-President had a brilliant mind, a fantastic memory and was a gifted writer.

Honors and degrees have come to Lowell Thomas in lavish profusion, and rightly so. His life story was reviewed on Ralph Edwards' TV program, *This is Your Life,* and the subject was completely taken aback by it all. A modest fellow, Lowell didn't cotton to the circus-barker atmosphere which Edwards created during these programs of surprise to the "victims."

Lowell Thomas is something of an athlete. His favorite sport is skiing, and he has developed a set of short skis, which have taken their famous owner down slopes in many resort areas.

In July, it was announced that the still-active broadcaster, at 88, is about to initiate a new syndicated radio show entitled *The Best Years.* In an interview he said, "When I started, I had the whole world to myself. Cronkite was nine, Brinkley was five, and Reasoner a two-year old. The test of today's newscasters weren't even born!"

"And, so long until tomorrow!"

FAMILY AUTOS

November 1980

Remember the first automobile you owned? How many have you had since then? If you can trace in chronological order your car purchases, it can reveal important milestones in your life.

Our family's first car was a matter of necessity and purchased early in the Depression. After father lost his job, due to the merging of the Buffalo, Rochester & Pittsburgh Railway with the Baltimore & Ohio in 1932, he was offered a position as auditor for Monroe County. This would entail his visiting the welfare officers in the 19 towns, so the securing of an automobile was mandatory. The last interurban trolleys had departed from this area the previous year, and suburban bus transportation was practically nonexistent.

On the advice of a friend, our family one Saurday afternoon visited the showrooms of Alling & Miles, the Hudson-Essex dealer at 82 Stone Street. Looking over the used cars, we spotted a black two-door 1929 Essex Super Six, and that became our means of transportation—for two days.

As father was in the process of learning to drive, Sunday afternoon we started out for a leisurely spin, Dad's oldest brother acting as instructor. We got two blocks from home and nearing a railroad crossing, Uncle Mike suddenly said, "Put on the brake!" Dad did and mother and I, who were in the back seat, almost

Five of the Klos Family Automobiles.

1929 Essex Super Six

1934 Pontiac Eight

1941 Buick Special

1953 Buick Special

1974 Pontiac LeMans

wound up in front! Mother was all for getting out then and there, but there were no rear doors, and Unc said tersely, "Sit down!"

We rode up Scottsville Road to a point near the river and turned around on a side road. Another thrill ensued as we started down a hill—backwards! That did it, as far as mother was concerned. What was needed was a four-door car for easy exit at times like that. But the writer was having the time of his life. Kids! They don't see the danger. They revel in ticklish situations.

The next afternoon, we were back at Alling & Miles, and spotted a four-door 1929 Essex Super Six, in black with natural wood spoke wheels, nickel-plated radiator, one windshield wiper, but certainly no radio, heater or defroster. Switching the license plates, 8M-92-94, we drove home.

That car was to serve us for about five years, and was driven over 70,000 miles. With no heater, an automobile robe was employed in the dead of winter, but it was still cold riding. In the beginning, every time the car hit major bumps, we thought the rattling of the tools behind the rear seat accounted for the unusual noise. After repeated stops to shift the tools and wrap them in cloth, a garageman told us that the noise was caused by the rear shock absorbers, and we couldn't do anything about it.

That car served faithfully as an instrument for Dad's work in auditing the welfare officers of the county. This was the era when localities attended to the needs of their poor and unemployed, not higher governmental authority as is the case now. Such names as Minnie Hugelmaier of Gates, Eli Hames of Webster, Edward Seward of Pittsford, William Martin of Irondequoit, Christie Pierce of Spencerport, Edward Dodd of Penfield, and Joseph Burke of Hamlin come to mind. The writer met all these and more, but our favorite was Mr. Dodd.

You see, his home was on Creek Street, on which there were scores of former interurban car bodies, used by farmers for various purposes. The Dodds had car No. 151 from the Rochester & Eastern Railway which was abandoned in 1930. The front part was used by Mrs. Dodd for her laundering, the rear for storage. The Redders down the road had No. 171 from the Rochester & Sodus Bay Railway, used as a fruit stand; Rochester & Eastern No. 162, and trackless trolley No. 319. Other car bodies dotted the landscape for years until vandals took their toll. We became fast friends of the Dodds!

We had a couple minor accidents with the Essex. On a stormy winter morning while driving the writer to school, we encountered two bicyclists, one on each side of the street. The one on the right fell, Dad flipped the wheel to avoid him, and the car made a 180-degree turn, smashing the rear left wheel against the curb, breaking it. A new wheel was purchased from Unit Parts, "The World of Auto Parts" on Main Street East.

Another time Dad didn't have the overhead door on the garage in its highest position and upon backing out, the car's fabric roof was torn loose. Still another time he forgot to close the rear door before entering the garage, and a fabric retainer was snapped. The most thrilling event for the writer occurred one cold winter evening when we were enroute home. On West Main Street the car hit an icy patch, and without warning, proceeded to make a 180-degree turn! Luckily no trolleys or other traffic were in the area to cause an accident.

When it came to shop for car number three, we visited the Clinton Auto Exchange in the 1200 block of North Clinton (where a supermarket and parking lot are located now). The dealer, a short fellow with an amusing accent, had a small showroom in front with repair facilities in the rear. We spotted a

1934 Pontiac four-door sedan in olive green, with spare tires in front fender wells, windshield ventilation wings, "knee action" front suspension, one windshield visor and a luggage rack in the rear. We took it on a demonstration spin one Sunday morning down to Kings Highway and got as far as Durand-Eastman Park.

It stalled on a hill, and before Dad could get it going (you didn't crank it; it had a electric starter button on the dash), it began backing down the hill! More thrills!

However, it became the family car and served Dad in his next job, district auditor for the New York State Welfare Department. His work took him to Elmira, Corning, Painted Post, Watkins Glen, Hornell, Bath, Belmont, Angelica, etc., and a lot of miles were covered with it. The engine was tuned so well that when waiting for a red light to change, one couldn't hear the eight cylinders idling. A friend who had received training in the Packard Automotive School paid the supreme compliment when he wondered if the engine were running. The car had no radio, but a heater, second windshield wiper and visor were installed.

One day when in the vicinity of Watkins Glen, there was a loud report and flash from the hood. A connecting rod had broken, necessitating a tow to the nearest garage. A call was made to the Pontiac factory and a new engine was on its way. General Motors supplied the engine, and Dad merely had to pay for the labor for installation, which wasn't much. The car was in use when the big Southern Tier flash flood struck in July, 1935. Dad got a rush call, ordering him to the area to help coordinate aid for the victims.

When the Pontiac's speedometer showed over 90,000 miles, it was decided to get a brand new car this time. The welfare officer of Hamlin, Joseph Burke, had a Buick agency, and always believing in the slogan, "When better automobiles are built, Buick will build them," we visited Burke's in October, 1940. There on the floor, some new 1941 Buicks were on display. One was a gun-metal gray, four-door special with radio, heater, luggage compartment, and what was called a "valve-in-head engine with twin carburetors." The last feature was to cause so much trouble that General Motors, at their expense, modified it on all models for better performance.

Then, on a Saturday afternoon, Mr. Burke took us for a spin in it. He turned on the radio and there was a play-by-play of the Cincinnati-Detroit World Series with Paul Derringer pitching against Dizzy Trout. This was living, we thought! The car rode like a dream and we were totally enthused with it. The purchase price? Would you believe $1100?

The Buick served faithfully through the war years and beyond. We like to think of it as the best car we owned. It had excellent workmanship and its riding qualities were unsurpassed. We had it the longest of any car, about 14 years. As in the case in areas where salt is used for ice control, the body was the first item to go, but the engine was still in good condition.

Car number five was a 1953 Buick special two-tone green, four-door sedan. But it wasn't in the same league as its predecessor. The workmanship wasn't as good, the car had been cheapened with lighter-guage steel and plastic. For a long time, gasoline fumes could be detected while riding and it was to plague us even with a new carburetor was installed. The car served the family until a new 1962 blue four-door Chrysler Newport replaced it.

This was a vast improvement over the previous car. It rode excellently, and was well-engineered, was our first car which didn't feature a manual gear shift. Push buttons on the dash were employed instead. As was the reason for replacing the Buicks, the body had rusted noticeably on the Chrysler, though the engine was still in excellent condition. There were only 22,000 miles on it!

When in the spring of 1974, we traded for a new four-door green Pontiac LeMans, we got a call from our old Chrysler's new owner, wondering why we had disposed of it. We assured him that there was nothing wrong, mechanically. Simply, the body had rusted too far for even extensive restoration, which would have been costly.

The Pontiac "Green Hornet" has given pretty faithful service, if one can overlook its tendency to stall before it is properly warmed up, especially in winter. This is due to the pollution control device with which all models were equipped in 1974. But, one learns quickly that no two automobiles run exactly alike. Each has its own personality, its own little idiosyncracies, just like a typewriter, a musical instrument, or a human being, for that matter.

If one thinks back to the cars he has owned, there will be many facets of his life which will come to mind in connection with them. It proves that the automobile, with which all Americans have fallen in love, has become as much a part of our lives as eating, sleeping, education and working. It has become an urgent necessity rather than a luxury.

The former "Kid From Brooklyn," now the "Sage of Olean, N.Y.," Doc Bebko. Theatre organist, chiropractor, world traveler, Jackie Gleason fan, story teller and philosopher has been a great friend of the author.

DOC BEBKO, MULTI-FACETED FRIEND

March, 1981

It is more than 21 years since we first shook hands with a fellow who impressed us with his prowess at a theatre pipe organ. Since that initial meeting, because of similar interests and beliefs, our acquaintance developed into an overriding friendship. The letters we've exchanged number in the hundreds.

His name is Dr. Edward J. Bebko, a highly successful Olean chiropractor, who was born in the shadow of the Brooklyn Bridge in 1910. He and his brothers, Gene, George and Ted, were typical American boys who pursued the normal things boys did in their youth.

And when we say "normal things," we don't mean smoking pot or getting into trouble with the law. We are prone to believe that if one of Pa Bebko's offspring strayed from the straight and narrow, a bit of corporal punishment would have been his reward. Needless to say, the Bebko brothers all achieved high status in their chosen professions, and now enjoy the fruits of their endeavors.

Music and the theatre were strong points in the Bebkos' lives. For example, George would come home every Saturday after viewing the weekly amateur night contests in Brooklyn's Halsey Street Theatre, saying, "That funny kid who emcees the acts looks even more funny when he comes out on the stage, dressed in a tuxedo several sizes too big. His hands almost disappear into his sleeves as he exchanges banter with his sidekick, Johnny Morgan."

The fellow in the oversize tux was none other than "The Golden Ham," or more readily known as "The Great One," Jackie Gleason. Johnny Morgan has been a friend of Jackie to this day, often appearing on his TV show. The comedian now has several closets of meticulously tailored apparel, labeled "big," "bigger," and "biggest," depending on his avoirdupois at the moment.

Doc Bebko became a theatre organist, playing a number of houses in the New York area, including the posh Harlem Opera House. His teachers were future Hall of Famers Frederick Kinsley, who played at the huge Hippodrome, and Don Baker, who performed at the Rialto, Rivoli, and later to spend almost 14 years at the "crossroads of the world," the New York Paramount Theatre. Doc adopted the professional name of Eddie Baker from his mentor.

One of the theatres in which he played was within a block of an amusement park. When his console stint was finished, he'd head there, flash his pass, and ride the roller coaster over and over. He still finds the sport exhilarating and on his travels has tried the one at Crystal Beach in Canada, a couple "mind-benders", and others. He's had to do this alone, as his wife, Stella, won't join her husband in these wild pursuits. Smart gal! The writer has a distaste for them too, a distaste which was implanted after a ride on the Sea Breeze Jack Rabbit in the thirties.

The roaring twenties must have been a great time as Doc can regale his friends with endless stores of the prohibition era, theatres, clubs, personalities, Ebbets Field, Yankee Stadium, etc. Of course, because of his many years spent in music as a livelihood, he can tell yarns of a few contemporaries, too. For example, the organist who played the RKO Chester Theatre was a South American, Raul de Toledo Galvao. He wisely simplified things by calling himself "Paul Brass." Doc was once invited to the Brass home and "treated" to a positively terrible meal. The meat was tough, the soup dishwater, the coffee not much better. Frequently, Brass ate his lunch in a nearby cemetery because it was "so nice and quiet." The bill of fare? Turkey legs.

Of course, Doc was a visitor to both the famous Roxy and New York Paramount theatres. At the latter, Mr. & Mrs. Jesse Crawford were presenting their duets and solos at the Wurlitzer's twin consoles. To this day, however, Doc insists that the fellow who caught his eye was Sigmund Krumgold, who accompanied the silent films. "Every Thursday the week's billing changed, and a lot of fellow organists attended the morning's first show which he played. I could learn more by hearing him than anyone. He was simply a master of his craft."

Doc's final tenure in a theatre was as third organist at the Radio City Music Hall from 1939 to 1941. He auditioned for chief organist Dick Leibert in the broadcasting studio, which has a small Wurlitzer of only 14 ranks. He must have been great, because Leibert said, "You open the first show tomorrow morning." The Music Hall organ happens to be one of 58 ranks, the largest Wurlitzer ever built.

Our subject married in November, 1941, and when he saw the handwriting on the wall for the diminshing theatre organ idiom, wisely took a course in chiropractic. He moved to Olean to be among the hills, scenery and fresh air, which were unknown in his Brooklyn years. Though he keeps his hand in by doing silent film shows (in the seventies he played silent classics at Buffalo's Museum of Science, and he's appeared for the Rochester Theater Organ Society several times), his very busy office schedule does not allow him time to prepare for formal concerts. "Give me a good silent comedy, a well-maintained and balanced pipe organ, and I'm in business," he says.

One couldn't find a truer American than Doc Bebko. He deplores the lack of patriotism, the lethargic response by some to the playing of our national anthem and to the display of the flag. The lack of common sense and fiscal responsibility on the part of those whom we have placed in all levels of government are sources of great worry to him.

"I thought I could retire at 65, but with this inflation, which is eating us alive, how can I?," he asks. Doc likes to travel, and why shouldn't he? He often puts in a 14-hour day at his office. Trips to his brothers, to his daughter Barbara and her family in Salt Lake City, sojourns to old haunts in New York, and an occasional cruise to the West Indies give the Bebkos something to look forward to. And he never fails to honor the writer with a postal card or two.

When Cimerama was popular in the sixties, Doc often came to Rochester and hosted us at the Monroe Theatre. Any revolutionary development in screen projection intrigues him. He also was witness to the birth (and death) of Smellovision in New York. "Odors suggested by the action on the screen were wafted into the auditorium; flower fragrances, soft coal, odors of the street, etc. However, the promoters killed their own goose by constructing a smoking booth in the rear of the house so the nicotine slaves could enjoy their habit while viewing the picture. The whole concept of Smellovision was lost to them."

Being connoisseurs of good motion pictures, the Bebkos frequently drive up to Buffalo where their son, Edward, is a theatre impressario. Edward started in the business by operating one house and now has several. He's anticipating the day when the new rapid transit line is completed, which will hopefully bring even more patrons to his downtown theatres, especially those from the University of Buffalo campus which the line will serve.

Doc Bebko works and lives in a very neat, well-maintained home a couple of blocks off Olean's Main Street. The white house stands amid towering trees, surrounded by a manicured carpet of rich, green lawn, and is so comfortably cool in the summer that one would believe it to be air conditioned. It is not.

In the opposite corners of the living room stand two giant Patrician speakers, and when a stereo steam train record is placed on the turntable, the resulting sound makes one feel that a locomotive is charging through! A cinema pipe organ record turns the room into a theatre auditorium. A Hammond with rhythm unit also graces the room. Doc is firmly in step with Jackie Gleason's belief; "That's the way to go." He buys nothing but the best and deservedly so.

In the adjoining sun parlor are Doc's memorabilia, records, tapes, turntables, and a beautiful celeste, once used by him in Harry Reser's orchestra. One the walls are autographed pictures of notables, posing with our subject.

Mrs. Bebko's domain is her neat all-electric kitchen, where she works her culinary magic. And what a cook! No turkey legs for her husband to eat in a cemetery! Our amazing friend eats well and wisely, and can tell at the drop of a hat which items are injurious to health. He has words of scorn for federal agencies, allegedly operating in the public's interest, which look the other way when it comes to confronting giant food processors, drug houses, etc.

Doc eats in the best restaurants while traveling. He told of his entering the late Toots Shor's emporium in New York. Shor just bellowed to the maitre d', "Hey, get these bums a table!"

Doc isn't too high on the fast-food outfits; he likes the atmosphere of formal dining plus the variety of beverages.

If he's in the New York area, chances are he'll drive his sleek Continental across the George Washington Bridge to Wanaque, New Jersey. There he makes for the Suburbian Restaurant, in which the ex-RKO Chester's Wurlitzer organ is used to entertain diners. When the house organist, Frank Cimmino, spies the good doctor, a special table is reserved for his party near the organ console, Doc is introduced, and he'll give forth with some wonderfully informal toe-tapping music for an hour or more. Selections such as *The Whip, Paramount on Parade,* and *Shuffle Off to Buffalo* get the diners into a bouncy mood. There is always a crowd to greet him afterwards.

Some years ago, Doc played a program, *Famous Fathers,* for a new York radio station, rubbing shoulders with Admiral Byrd, Howard Lindsay, Harry Langdon, Lauritz Melchoir, Lowell Thomas, Morton Downey and Eddie Cantor. This experience introduced him to some of the true gentlemen of America. To this day, he idolizes Lowell Thomas (as do we). "The man is utterly fantastic. No one can touch him as a newscaster. As an authority on all areas of the world, he's seen them all. And at his age, he can still put present newscasters to shame."

Doc Bebko has a strong vein of humor which can lighten any conversation. His favorite silent movie comedians were W. C. Fields, Harry Langdon, Laurel & Hardy, and Charlie Chaplin. Of today's crowd, he singles out Peter Sellers, George Burns, Jackie Gleason and Benny Hill.

Above all, Doc is a gentleman's gentleman. He is solicitious of his friends and a joy in any conversation. Never at a loss for words, he doesn't infuse his speech with "ya know" or "OK" in every other phrase while his thinking power catches up to his speech.

It was a great event that Sunday morning in January, 1960, when we were introduced by mutual friend, Jess Littlefield, to Doc Bebko, who appropriately was seated at the organ console in Buffalo's Roosevelt Theatre. And it has been a great day whenever we've been in his company, have received a letter from him, or conversed on the telephone.

My life has been incalculably enriched by this friendship.

Rochester's fire horses

Exercising the team in Maplewood Park

The parade nears the Four Corners

FAITHFUL FIRE HORSES

July 1981

Had you been in the vicinity of 218 Main Street East around 11:30 a.m. on February 16, 1927, you'd have witnessed an historical moment in Rochester, the last of a familiar sight which never failed to quicken the pulse. Three charging horses, pulling a water tower, galloped up Main Street hill from Fire Headquarters on Central Avenue to answer an alarm for an insignificant fire in a cloak store.

Thereafter, all alarms of fire would be answered by motor-driven fire apparatus; Rochester's Fire Department had become completely motorized, a process which took 18 years. The horses were relegated to light duty or to pasture on the SPCA farm.

Before 1861, fire-fighting in the city was done by hand-pumped equipment, brought to the blaze by the firemen themselves. In that year, the city acquired two horse-drawn steamers and, unable to hire suitable horses, the city bought them. At first the steeds were used for other jobs as well, but this had to be abandoned. Work horses did not make good fire horses. By 1863 the city had 12 fire horses, four steam engines, and four hose carts. In 1887, as the city grew, there were 30 horses.

The fire horses, averaging 1400 pounds, were the elite of the equine population. Only the finest animals which came into the market were purchased. Since they had to operate as a unit, they were carefully trained to make sure that not only did each pull his weight, but also wasn't overeager, thereby destroying the rhythm of the team. All fire horses had three things in common: They had to have stamina and wind to endure the fast runs, and they had to be well-mannered to respond instantly to commands. It usually took 10 days to two weeks to train a fire horse.

Hitching the animals for a run was an act in itself. As soon as the fire bell rang, they dashed from their stalls and took their places in front of the equipment. The harness was dropped onto them by an overhead apparatus, cinched by firemen, and with the doors open, off they went in a matter of seconds.

While racing to a fire, the greatest dangers were the horse cars and other horse-drawn rigs. Occasionally a horse would throw a shoe, and it is recorded that the fire chief once paid a North Street woman 60 cents for a broken window, caused by a flying horseshoe.

There was a standing rule that upon returning to the firehouse, the animals had to be thoroughly rubbed down and dried. They represented a costly investment, as well as minutes in getting to a fire. Not only were the horses meticulously groomed, but the harness and other items of tack were tirelessly cleaned. The brass was shined to mirror brilliance. The steam engines, ladder wagons and hose carts were maintained in like fashion. The engines, while awaiting a call, were always ready with five pounds of steam pressure, an oilsoaked brand ready for lighting.

In the winter, three horses pulled the engines and ladder wagons, two on the hose carts. In the summer, each team was one horse fewer. Upon reaching the fire scene, the horses were unhitched and led away, obviating any injury or discomfort.

On February 26, 1904, however, the horses had an additional function. On that date Rochester had its most destructive and memorable conflagration on Main Street East, between St. Paul

Waiting for the Annual Parade to begin

A ladder company parades down Main Street

An Engine Company parades on Main Street near Water

A parade, eastbound on Main Street at Fitzhugh

and Clinton, otherwise known as "The Sibley Fire." With the entire north side of Main threatened with destruction, fire apparatus was rushed here from Syracuse and Buffalo on railroad flatcars. The local fire horses were driven to the railroad and hitched to the apparatus which was pulled to the fire scene.

However, the apparatus couldn't be connected to Rochester's fire hydrants. The officials in their haste forgot that the hose couplings were of a different size. So the out-of-town engines pumped water from a nearby raceway. This incident resulted in a state law standardizing the size of all fire-hose and hydrant couplings. This contingency also occurred during a major fire in Baltimore the same year, and Maryland enacted similar legislation.

Every year the Rochester Fire Department had an annual parade and inspection. The well-groomed horses, the shiny apparatus, and the firemen in Class A uniforms with white gloves, paraded proudly down Main Street, past the reviewing stand where the mayor, city commissioners, and other dignitaries took the salutes. There was much pride on the part of the firemen in those days to keep their equipment in top condition. With inspections and parades, there was no time to become lethargic with the condition of men, beasts and machines. During the 1901 parade, the city hall bell rang, signifying a fire. The horses tugged and off they ran to the fire scene. No white-gloved salutes for the politicians that day!

In 1907, a horseshoeing rig was organized and made the rounds of all the firehouses. Before that, local blacksmiths did the job. In the rear of Engine 10 on Driving Park Avenue was the hospital for fire horses. Albert Tegg and his two sons administered to the needs of the animals.

February 1, 1909, marked a milestone in the history of the Rochester Fire Department. Chief Little made a trial run in the first auto used by a fire chief here. On April 20, 1912, the first piece of mechanized apparatus, a Pope-Hartford combination chemical and hose cart, was put into service at Hose 3 in Plymouth Avenue North. The horses' days were numbered, and for the next 15 years they were systematically replaced by motor-driven vehicles.

Following the last run in 1927, the city saw six teams of them in a parade that July in Fire Horse Day. A memorial tablet, presented by the American Legion, was accepted for the city by Mayor Martin B. O'Neil. Until the early fifties, it stood at the Court Street side of the City Hall Annex. When demolition of that building for the Community War Memorial occurred, the tablet was removed to Cobbs Hill and placed near the fire-police radio station. The plaque reads:

"Our fire horses, glorious in beauty and in service. Faithful friends, we cannot call them dumb, because they spoke in deeds in every hour of danger. Perpetual remembrance enshrines their loyalty and courage." The figures on the plaque were copied from the picture of three horses and a steam engine in Maplewood Park, racing to a mythical fire.

The fire horses with the longest terms of service at the time of their retirement in 1927 were Brown Bobby of Engine 17 on Stillson Street, appointed in 1910; Little Chubby, Engine 6, University Avenue, December 1910; Grey Dick, Engine 8, Gregory Street, 1912; Big Tom, Hose 21, Genesee and Barton Streets, 1913; and Black Dick, Engine 16, Hudson Avenue and Bernard Street, 1913.

Little Chubby once had a miraculous escape from death. While racing with a hose cart through Clifton Street in answer to a box alarm, the driver tried to turn the rig into Prospect Street when the reins broke. The unguided team tore straight across Prospect, jumped the curb, smashed through a picket fence and broke down the door of a cottage. One horse was half way up the stairs before being stopped. Chubby, thought to be dead, was lying under the debris, but fortunately, escaped with small cuts. The stair-climbing equine had to receive treatment at the veterinary hospital.

By 1931, Little Chubby was spending his retirement at the SPCA animal shelter in Scottsville. One night a small fire broke out there, and the Scottsville Fire Department responded, an old-time fire gong ringing on one of its vehicles. Chubby perked up his ears, pranced about, and acted as if he were to answer the call again.

It was a thrill-provoking sight to see the magnificant fire horses at full speed, pulling a shiny piece of apparatus. It was a thrill akin to that of seeing a steam-powered locomotive charge by.

St. Paul-Summerville Trolley Line

#865 at St. Paul loop near the city line.

#866 inbound from Summerville near the city line.

#868 at Summerville loop.

TROLLEYS TO SUMMERVILLE

October 1982

Though it passed into history more than 43 years ago, memories are still vivid of the Summerville trolley line. Walking on the St. Paul Boulevard sidewalks, it's easy to envision a trolley's lumbering over the tracks which preceded the macadam walks.

Prior to 1894, there was a steam line in the area, the Rochester & Lake Ontario Belt Railroad, built about 1883. It ran from Avenue D northward, across St. Paul Street and along the Genesee River bank, then eastward to Windsor Beach. The first train carried 1500 passengers. Part of the line's success was attributed to the activities at Rifle Range (now lower Seneca Park), Brinker's Race Track and the picnic grounds nearby. Also, the previous year, the Windsor Beach Pavilion was built. Often called "The House of Glass," it was declared by many to be the finest summer resort structure in western New York. The builders and proprietors were Frank Firtzsche, Joseph Stallknecht and Sol Wile.

At this time, Irondequoit was a sparsely settled town. No one lived north of Stutson Street or in Summerville or Windsor Beach in the winter. Even the life-saving crew (not called "Coast Guard" then) departed from its lakeside station with advent of the first snowfall, returning in the spring. St. Paul (or Summerville) Boulevard was known sometimes as East Side

Boulevard and ended at a swamp where Bengal's Inn was located.

Farms and peach orchards occupied most of the land from Ridge Road to the lake. The only thoroughfares leading off St. Paul Boulevard were East Road or "Little Ridge" (now Titus Avenue), Hudson Avenue (Cooper Road), Sherry Road (Pinegrove Avenue) and Smuggler's Road, later River Road (Thomas Avenue).

St. Paul Boulevard's first pavement was of clay and gravel, hauled from the Rifle Range area by the Ira M. Ludington Co. in 1893. Oddly, a large tree was left standing in the center of the thoroughfare near Cole Road. The Rochester & Irondequoit Turnpike Company had a two-story frame tollgate house on the east side of the boulevard opposite the Hosea Rogers property, and another tollgate at the Cooper Road intersection.

After the first improvement to the boulevard, mileposts were installed on the east side of the road for bicyclists to measure time and speeds. Members of bicycle clubs such as the Lakeview Wheelmen, Seneca Wheelmen, and Newport Cycle Club raced down the road.

In May, 1983, four years after the first electric trolley in Rochester ran from Lake Avenue and Ridge Road to Charlotte, the Rochester & Irondequoit Railway was organized. Max Brickner was president; W. D. Ellwanger, secretary; and Frederick P. Allen, treasurer. The aim of the new company was to build a trolley line from the city limits (Ridge Road then) to Summerville. It purchased 17–foot strips on both sides of St. Paul Boulevard, and an 80–foot wide strip from Cole Road to the lake for about a mile, which provided direct access to the Summerville-Charlotte ferry. The railway's office was at Summerville.

The line was opened in 1894. A subsidiary, the Windsor

Beach Improvement Company, purchased the land there and at Summerville, mostly from the Bietry farm. A hotel was built at Windsor Beach, streets laid out and trees planted. Near the ferry landing, a pavilion, "The Round House," was built. Traction companies frequently purchased real estate near lakes and bays, then developed amusement parks and hotels on the sites, making them accessible by extending their trolley lines. Net earnings of the Summerville line's first year of operation was $21,371.

Given the pleasures of the lakeside resorts, plus the opportunity to take the ferry (the "Yosemite," later the "Windsor") to Charlotte, "Western New York's Coney Island," the Summerville trolley line was most successful in the days before the automobile.

Dr. Dexter Perkins, Rochester city historian, in 1941 wrote:

> We can hardly realize what an important agency of amusement and recreation the trolley was in the nineties. The streetcar company itself constantly urged upon the people of Rochester the desirability of seeing the sights of the city and the lakeshore in this elegant vehicle. It set up a lively competition with the steam railroad in transporting passengers to Charlotte. It pointed out that its cars were "open, clean, and filled with Ontario's ozone-laden air," while the train gave the passengers the appearance of "having delivered coal."
>
> It built lines to Summerville and Windsor Beach which the railroad did not reach, and offered round-trip tickets for 25 cents, 15 cents on Sundays. It advertised its merits in poetry, which was perhaps a little short of Miltonic, but which had its appeal nonetheless. Here are a couple rhymes of the time:
>
> Come, boys and girls of every age,
> Get ready for a lark,
> And take a trolley ride with me
> To Sea Breeze Park.
>
> or

To stay in town these red hot days,
To say the least is tough;
So take a car to Windsor Beach
And lunch upon the bluff.

Here was a means of transportation unrivaled in its day for the great body of citizens of our city.

For its first 10 years, the Summerville trolley line operated in the summer months only. To guarantee year-round service, Irondequoit resident L. P. Gunson purchased $500 worth of tickets in 1905 and resold them to people living along the route.

In 1895, the Windsor Beach Pavilion fire occurred, which caused a subsequent drop in trolley revenues. In 1900, the road was acquired through auction by the Rochester & Suburban Railway Company, which also ran the Sea Breeze line from Portland Avenue and Bay Street to the east side resort. A serious accident was recorded in 1902 when a collision of two trolleys at a tollgate on Summerville Boulevard injured 15. With consolidation of Rochester city lines by the Rochester Railway Company accomplished in 1905, the Rochester & Suburban was absorbed by the mother company. Five years later, the tollgates on the boulevard were dismantled. By then the automobile began its inexorable rise to popularity. In preparation for it, St. Paul Boulevard received its first asphalt surface in 1915.

Merged into the newly-formed New York State Railways in 1912, the Summerville line continued to be a popular means of transit for lakeside-bound travelers, and for Irondequoiters who built homes in tracts which were carved out of the large farms. The writer and his family made many a trip to Summerville for afternoons of fishing or boat-watching on the federal pier. The size of the lake craft had a wider range than the mere yacht club inhabitants of today. The Ontario Car Ferries, the Charlotte-to-

Sea Breeze steamers, naval reserve subchaser SC-433, Coast Guard patrol boat CG-2280 and white picket boat, coal carriers, etc., have all departed the scene.

In July 1929, plans were announced for the further improvement of St. Paul Boulevard. Included was the elimination of the trolley line, and the purchase of the right-of-way for $100,000. Also, the boulevard residents petitioned for bus substitution and a 10-cent fare, which meant no additional charge north of the city line. The city was asked to approve the plan, as it would have removed $450,000 from the $20 million valuation of the local lines. Still, the city had to guarantee six percent return under terms of the service-at-cost contract with the utility.

However, James F. Hamilton, New York State Railways president, emphatically stated that no bus substitution would occur and the company would fight any such plan. It was to take almost 10 years for the firm's successor, Rochester Transit Corp., to about-face on this no-substitution policy.

By 1931, the 4.5–mile St. Paul Boulevard was completely rebuilt. Gasoline-powered shovels, chain-drive dump trucks and steam rollers were used in the project. Dolomite was used for the road base, hauled from Gates quarries. Track relocation was done beneath the two railroad bridges near the lake. Cost was $300,000, with each abutting property owner assessed $10 per running foot.

In 1936 sodium vapor lights were introduced, the third installation in the country. A parade on July 29 heralded the lighting of the "Path of Gold." Cost of this was $16,000.

The Summerville trolley line was prone to accidents and service disruptions the year round. Its history was marked by numerous derailments which sent the emergency truck careening down the boulevard, its siren screaming. A derailment or a tree blown down onto the tracks would tie up the single-track line until the repair crews worked their magic. A faded clipping, dated June 19, 1936, tells us that a truck turned into the path of a trolley at Belcoda Drive. The motorman, seeing the impending accident, set the trakes and jumped toward the rear of the car. The front vestibule was smashed but there were no injuries.

On January 20, 1937, 12 passengers escaped serious injury when a Summerville-bound trolley derailed at the edge of a 50–foot drop (still there) near Pinegrove Avenue. The car was proceeding slowly after discharging a passenger, else it would have slid down the embankment. The car's front hung over the depression. Northbound traffic was blocked for an hour until the wrecking crew worked the car back onto the track.

In winter, cars often got stuck in snowdrifts, as wide-open spaces prevailed before the area became a residential community. For light snow, sweepers were used. Flange plows and rotaries were employed for drifts.

On February 10, 1939, the Irondequoit Democratic Town and County Committee asked Supervisor Thomas E. Broderick and the Town Council to force the Rochester Transit Corporation to clear its Summerville tracks of snow. An exceptionally heavy snowstorm the previous week triggered this action. The company had made an attempt to keep the line open, but when a plow derailed, buses were stubbed from the city line to the lake with many delays. The committee's resolution also asked the Supervisor and Council to assure residents of adequate service before granting the RTC permission to operate buses in St. Paul Boulevard to replace the trolleys.

The RTC's obsession under president John Uffert was for complete substitution of trolleys with buses on all lines, and the late thirties saw the wholesale replacement of the loyal streetcar. The Summerville line was doomed.

On May 22, 1939, shortly after midnight, a sizeable crowd,

ignoring the early morning chill, gathered at Summerville to await the arrival of the last trolley. Supervisor Broderick, town officials, Irondequoit Centennial committeemen, and transit officials met earlier at the St. Paul Exempt Firemen's Home on Thomas Avenue. They rode by bus to the city line, transferred to the trolley, piloted by Herbert Singleton, and rode to Summerville. They returned by 18–passenger bus to the Exempts for an early-morning breakfast.

Empty, the last trolley trundled slowly along the familiar roadbed for the last time—this was the final run. Clever devices sprouted on the overhead trolley wire which caused dewirement several times and a large sign had been thrown across the rails at one location.

Forty buses replaced 25 trolleys on the Summerville route. Shortly after, ties, rails and overhead were removed and sidewalks of macadam were laid in the trolley roadbed. Thus, the Summerville trolley line faded into the wings of history in the year of the Irondequoit Centennial. It was a loyal friend of Irondequoiters and merrymakers alike for 45 years.

Dr. William E. Dake, whose remedies included a liberal dose of friendship.

DOC DAKE
MEDICINE WITH FRIENDSHIP

May 1983

In recent years, much has been said about the new breed of medical doctor. In the past, he was called "the family physician." Nowadays, the present model seems bent on being a specialist in one form of medicine or the other.

A doctor who deserves a special salute took care of this writer from infancy until the physician died after World War II. He was the infant specialist, Dr. William Embury Dake, and of all the physicians who've attended to our aches, pains and ills, it was Doc Dake whom this writer admired most of all.

Dr. Dake was recommended by a family friend sometime after my brother, Floyd, was born in November, 1920. Floyd, injured by instruments at birth, was never well, crying much of the time. Several doctors were engaged. One, upon being summoned, came into the house and his first question was not a solicitious query about the patient, but "Any calls for me?" He was dismissed shortly after.

Finally, Dr. Dake provided the honest answers which the others were evading for months. "Mother and Dad," he said, "your baby never will be well," and proceeded to explain why. "The best you can do," he said, "is to make him comfortable," and recommended placing him during the hot summer of 1921 in the

Infant Summer Hospital (later Convalescent Hospital for Children) on Beach Avenue. Floyd died there shortly after.

When the writer checked in at 10 pounds, 9 ounces in December, 1922, everything seemed perfect. However, five and a half weeks later, an operation was mandatory. The passage from the stomach to the intestine had closed. Dr. Dake recommended the surgeon, Dr. Searle Sumner, for the delicate task. It was successful, but this infant was so weak that he couldn't be moved from the operating table for hours. Dr. Dake told Mother straight from the shoulder, "Your baby is going to be pretty ill for several months, but he will recover if you follow my instructions."

To Mother's everlasting credit, she followed Dr. Dake's wishes to the letter in regard to infant formula and diet. If the measure said two and a half ounces, that's what was given. Much of the time the stomach refused to accept food simply because of its tender state. It was discouraging to have the food rejected, especially after the putting on of fresh clothing minutes before. But after several months when the stomach became stronger and the food stayed down, I came on like gangbusters! It took five months to regain the same weight as at birth. Good thing I checked in at 10–9!

Of course, Doc Dake looked us over periodically. In those days his office was a large converted house at 237 Alexander Street; later he moved to the Medical Arts Building. We especially enjoyed the trip as it meant riding the serpentine Park Avenue trolley line. Mother once asked Doc if he were to buy a pet for his children would he buy a dog or cat. He preferrd the canine to the feline, and our resulting collie was a great companion for years.

It was in the summer of 1929 that another crisis arose with this writer. A mason who was cutting a driveway at our old home carelessly left his tools in a pail on a step below the entrance to the back door. Not seeing this, I stepped out into a blade of a trowel. The resulting gash in my right leg had blood spurting onto the floor.

Not losing her head, Mother put me into a chair, got the leg up, laid cold cloths over the wound and called Dr. Dake. He sent his surgeon, who stopped the bleeding by inserting several clamps, then gave a dose of anti-tetanus. As later events proved, it was an overdose, and coupled with the hot, muggy July weather, it resulted in a maniac attitude and a feeling of being on fire. I couldn't have water for 24 hours. Most efforts of relief failed until Recreo Powder was applied, causing me to drop off to sleep. It was the one time in life when this writer felt very close to death. Dr. Dake, however, saw me through the crisis.

In the fall, Dr. Dake vacationed at Baileys Bay, Bermuda. He sent a card, which I still treasure, signed "Your sincere friend, Dr. W. E. Dake."

Before entering school, I was free from the normal childhood diseases. Through serum, such maladies as scarlet fever and diphtheria were being relegated into oblivion. I did become ill in the fall of 1929, Dr. Dake diagnosing it as a change from upland Hemlock Lake water to Lake Ontario water when we moved to Irondequoit. Once in school, I contacted measles twice and whooping cough. All mother had to do was to call Doc Dake, and shortly after, depending on his schedule, he'd pay us a house call. In those days it was only $5, but it was reassuring to the family to have this tall, broad-shouldered, well-dressed man enter this patient's room.

"How are you doing, fellow?" was his greeting. Then out came the thermometer; then the cold stethoscope with its attendant probing. Also, the hated tongue depressor. "Keep him in bed for a couple of days, and give him these tablets with a lot of water," were his instructions. In no time I'd be up and back to school, thanks to the ministrations of Dr. Dake.

When father was employed as chief accountant of the Buffalo, Rochester & Pittsburgh Railway Company, the firm distributed some high-class calendars each year—ones you could read at a considerable distance. The printing was white on a black background. Dr. Dake always asked for one to use in his office.

I recall some of our Saturday afternoon visits to Dr. Dake's office in the Medical Arts Building, and they weren't hurried affairs. After the usual examination, weight and height checks, blood samples, etc., we'd sit and talk for awhile. On one occasion the Great Depression and its effect on local industry were discussed. In late September, 1934, knowing Doc's interest in sports, I asked who'd win the World Series between the Cardinals and the Tigers. "The Cards," said he. "With the Dean brothers pitching, how could they do otherwise?" The Cardinals became World Champions that fall.

Around Christmastime for years, like clockwork, I came down with what was called "intestinal grippe." Perhaps it was a spin-off of the infant operation. The last time was in December, 1936, and I barely managed to get through the school assembly program on the last day prior to the holiday vacation. In fact, there was but one year of the 12 during grammar and high school that I was able to achieve perfect attendance—the seventh grade. And that was the year they decided to eliminate giving of attendance pins! Principal Maude I. West of Hosea Rogers School explained that too many kids were coming to school with ailments just to get the pins, causing their classmates to be exposed to their illnesses.

For the winter months and decreased sunshine, Doc Dake prescribed Patch's Flavored Cod Liver Oil. A spoonful after each meal was the dosage. It may sound a bit distasteful, but this "bottled sunshine," as it was advertised, did seem to prevent colds by keeping up bodily resistance to them.

Doc Dake had good recommendations for fever or sore throat. For the former, it was Sweet Spirits of Nitre, and for the latter, a mixture of honey and lemon. They never failed to work wonders. This, you remember, was before the days of extensive use of aspirin.

When it was time to enter the service in World War II, I paid Doc Dake, then at 83 Culver Road, a visit for a final examination and to say goodbye. He agreed to drop in and visit the folks during my absence. He kept his promise and with his wife, paid Mother a call one afternoon. "Here is one home in which you never see a speck of dust," he told Mr. Dake. It was a deserved compliment to my fastidious mother.

The last time I saw Doctor Dake was on a Sunday afternoon in 1948. I was enroute to watch friends at a softball game at Cobbs Hill. I stopped and talked briefly with the good doctor and his wife, who were seated on their porch overlooking the park. He died not long after.

Thanks to his daughter, Margaret, who trained as a nurse at Genesee Hospital, we were able to secure the accompanying photo of Dr. William E. Dake. He was a true family doctor, a humanitarian, and a wonderful person to know.

The Crescent Beach Restaurant as it looks today, Western New York's mecca for great dining and atmosphere.

REBIRTH OF THE CRESCENT BEACH HOTEL

February 1984

Like the Phoenix which rose from its ashes, the new Crescent Beach Restaurant is serving the public in an aura of splendor, which makes it a reborn "Riviera of the East." As one who had a feeling of extreme sadness when the predecessor lakeside landmark was destroyed by fire in February, 1973, that feeling was replaced by exultation following the opening of the new restaurant last September.

As long as elderly residents can remember, there has been a hotel or restaurant at 1372 Edgemere Drive in Greece. The first was George Pangborn's small hotel, which was in operation before the turn of the century. About 1900, the first Crescent Beach Hotel was built by Win H. Lewis, a motorman on the Rochester & Manitou Railroad, which ran past the site. It was a two-story wooden frame building with porches on two sides.

Later, the structure was replaced by a much larger building, the nucleus of the hotel which burned in 1973. The place had lodging for 21 guests, and was the 10th stop on the R&M. Ownership later passed to the Erhmantrout family, Leon Erhmantrout operating it from 1930 to 1945. It grew into one of the most popular and profitable restaurants in the entire metropolitan Rochester area.

In 1945, the Crescent Beach Hotel was purchased by Raymond V. and Lorraine Geis. A former cosmetics salesman and purchaser of real estate, Mr. Geis' advent into the restaurant business presaged even bigger things for the establishment. Lorraine said they hadn't planned to enlarge the hotel. "Ray was reluctant to add on, but the heavy patronage demanded it."

Beginning in 1948, it was extensively remodeled. The dining capacity was increased from 90 to 450, and the decor became French-mid-Victorian. When the place was closed during the winter, usually between November 15 to March 15, the Geises took a vacation, but their establishment was not forgotten. "We would completely redecorate after closing every year," says Lorraine. "We bought outdoor lights from the Firestone Estate in Miami when the Fountainbleu Hotel was built on the site, chandeliers from the Edsel Ford Estate, and candelabra from Venice. We also went to the Bigelow factory to choose carpeting which would blend into the French-Victorian decor."

The couple also visited quaint shops to purchase artifacts, statuary and other items. Among the best remembered decorations was the beautiful white wrought iron, which surrounded the hotel and which supported the green canopy at the main entrance. Near the lounge was a ceiling-to-floor simulated waterfall.

What once was a little summer resort place became a famous landmark for fine dining. The writer's good friends, Dr. and Mrs. Edward J. Bebko of Olean, for example, always liked to dine in the Crescent Beach Hotel atmosphere when in town several times a year. Mr. and Mrs. Milton Sauer ate there every evening, at the same table, served by the same waitress. On Fridays, readers of the local papers were reminded of the place through homey ads with cute jingles, such as "Eat and play with Lorraine and Ray." They urged the reader to "eat in our beautiful lakefront dining room," and ended with "Your hosts, Lorraine and Ray Geis."

The writer remembers Mr. Geis quite well. While working at the Charlotte office of the old Genesee Valley Union Trust Co. in 1956, Ray came in every afternoon with the previous day's receipts, always in the several-thousand-dollar range. Quite often he'd call a produce dealer and order the next day's provisions. According to Mr. Joseph Barry, the present owner, "Ray loved to get away for awhile and perform these daily chores; it was a means of relaxation for him. His station wagon always returned to the hotel, loaded solidly."

It was a local journalist, G. Curtis Gerling, who stated in his review of fine dining places in his book, *Good Enough for Grandpa,* that "if you had to choose between buying the U. S. Mint and the Crescent Beach Hotel, take Cresent Beach."

The bottom line of the place's success was that top quality meals were served for the family trade at affordable prices, with excellent service. The nightly entertainment was varied, usually beginning at nine. Organist Bernie George, Piano Pasha, Hank Burger and his Dixieland Ramblers, singer Arline Daniels and pianist Sara Contine had multiple-week segments. The orchestras of Kenny Unwin and Sammy Stiles are also remembered.

The Crescent Beach Hotel could be booked for banquets, picnics, parties, etc. The old Board of Supervisors' annual picnic, a breezy affair, was held there in the summer, usually after a monthly noon meeting. Supervisor Gordon A. Howe and Sheriff Albert W. Skinner, both from Greece, led the parade of officials, politicians and media representatives through the canopied entrance.

In 1946, Joseph Barry came to the Crescent Beach Hotel as a bartender. Words cannot express the admiration he had for Ray Geis. "His head was never larger than the place; the place was never larger than his head," he recalls. "He was simply the most wonderful man to work for and besides idolizing him, I learned much by studying his methods of operation. Ray had to be one of the finest men I ever knew." When Ray became ill and decided to retire in 1965, Joe was able to take over and keep the staff intact. "I could have sold to out-of-town buyers, but I wanted to keep it in the family," Ray said. The Geises moved to Florida and the Barrys made the enterprise a real family affair. Joe, his wife Gloria, and their four sons, Chris, Mike, Mark and Jeff, worked in various capacities.

Architecturally, the Crescent Beach Hotel didn't change under the new ownership. A few thousand lights were added, the patio and lawn areas were re-landscaped. The clientele continued to come, some from other states and Canada. The restaurant served 1200 dinners on a good day, more than its predecessor served in a year! A staff of 120 was employed in 1972.

Fire started in the mostly-wood building February 11, 1973. When firemen arrived, the blaze had developed into an inferno whose fiery glare could be seen for miles. A caretaker who lived on the third floor died in the blaze. Joe Barry received the shocking news in Florida. "It was devastating," he said.

To visit the site and see nothing but ice-encrusted rubble was a painful experience to those of us who had been patrons. Clientele, friends of the family, even the younger Barrys urged reconstruction. In the interim, they ran Barry's Party House on Dewey Avenue, but it was no replacement for Crescent Beach.

On April 19, 1978, an item in the press stirred our attention: "Restaurant at Crescent Beach May be Rebuilt on Same Site." An application to rebuild, "recreating the setting to what it once was," was filed with the Greece Town Board by Jeff Barry. A public hearing a couple of months later was favorable, the area residents approving the rebuilding in a survey.

After all the necessary preliminaries which took time in this sophisticated age, ground-breaking ceremonies were held on February 2, 1983, with town and county officials present. A power shovel started removing debris, old trees and bushes, before digging the basement. In the months which followed, the writer and hundreds of others were frequent visitors to the site as the new and greater Crescent Beach Restaurant took shape. It was an exciting seven months, not unlike witnessing the building of a ship or skyscraper.

While the new edifice was under construction, someone apparently felt the pangs of guilt. Following the fire, people descended upon the site like vultures. Outdoor lights, flagstones from the patio, and much of the beautiful wrought iron were ripped out and carted away by scavengers.

One night, at least a ton of the wrought iron was returned. With it was a handwritten note of apology, a clipping from the Moody Bible Institute and a religious verse. Someone had mended his errant ways and returned that which was not his. Wrought iron is very expensive, and the Barrys were most appreciative of the turn of this item which had been so much a part of the exterior decor. It will be reinstalled as will a Blessed Mother shrine and fountain.

When September, 1983, arrived, the opening day was in sight and the newspaper ads proudly proclaimed it for Friday, September 16. The place was packed, floral pieces from well-wishers decorated the vestibule, and there was an air of excitement. Mr. Barry told the writer of several persons who had tears in their eyes, so happy were they of the resurrection. "One lady held my hand so tightly that I wondered if she'd ever let go, as she recalled happy times spent on the site years previously," he said. The new Crescent Beach Hotel had arrived!

The reconstruction cost more that $500,000 and included

razing three neighboring houses for additional parking space. More will be necessary, because even before the opening, Mr. Barry had plans to double the size of the dining room. Now it seats about 200 diners a la carte and 285 banquet-style. It has mirrors on the south wall to reflect the lake, which is no more than 25 feet from the building, and 12 large picture windows on the north side.

The walls are painted a soft pink, mixed to complement the light reflected from the lake. "It is a tremendous compliment to human skin complexion, also," according to architect Peter Morse. Actually, this feature was carried over from the old building, according to Mrs. Geis, who was responsible for decorating the new establishment. "We used a lot of pink in the ceilings to get a 'mauvey' look. Women liked that rosy light because it made them look well. If you can keep women happy, they'll bring their husbands or gentlemen friends," she said.

There are three large brass and crystal chandeliers for evening-hour lighting. The carpeting is thick and flowery to compliment the pink and gold which dominate the dining room, lounge and bar area. Crystal-clear mirrors and a shelf of 50 miniature dolls, some animated, surround the bar. Muted rose-colored tapestries from Italy hang in gilt-edge frames high on the dining room walls.

The ladies' rest room is reminiscent of a 19th entury French boudoir, with silk wall hangings, a full-length mirror, and ornate Victorian-style lamps. In the men's room, the walls are adorned with Norman Rockwell sketches. On the second floor is a sizeable banquet/party room. Easy access to the building for wheelchair patrons is provided by a concrete ramp.

The future? Besides doubling the size of the dining room, Mr. Barry says there will be more fountains and floral items added to the enlarged garden area to the east and to the patio which is on the lake side. Once the outside landscaping is finished, postal cards will be available to entice the populace to visit the new "Riviera of the East." But he emphasizes that this will be done over a period of years. After all, the Crescent Beach Hotel, like Rome, was not built in a day.

One of the place's priceless assets is a lady who has long been with the establishment, Ann Torpey. A person with an engaging personality, a fantastic memory and a golden gift for making one welcome, she greets guests at the coat-checking facility. She has also been responsible for much of the flower gardens surrounding the place, which attest to her multiple talents. Mrs. Torpey "goes with the franchise."

Barry's philosophy of operation is: "Serve the best food, provide impeccable service, and keep the prices down through high business volume. I believe that people are hungry for a place they can show off while entertaining. Our restaurant encourages people to circulate and mingle. They enjoyed this in the old days, as everybody knew everybody else.

"The new menu, like that of the old place, has something for everybody, from steaks and chops to Italian specialties, with roasts and other homey-type entrees on Sundays. Prices are modest, and on weekdays 'early-bird' specials are featured.

"It's like a dream, a feeling of nostalgia, a return to the pages of history. We believe the minute the people walk through the doors, they'll have that feeling of brought-back memories," he said.

The restaurant has been open throughout the winter. "I can't wait for the spring and summer seasons to begin. It is something I've anticipated for a long time, and it will be great to have the good weather to bring folks out to see us," the proud owner said.

This writer, having sampled the excellent food and facilities of the new Crescent Beach Hotel, unhestitatingly affixes his stamp of approval. He joins thousands of area citizens in wishing the Barry family the ultimate of success in their new venture. Determination and perseverance over adversity have their rewards, and the Barrys deserve everything which is good.

PALMYRA'S FAMOUS SAILOR SON

July 1985

When the United States becme a world power with the defeat of Spain in the "splendid little war" of 1898, as diplomat John Hay so aptly described it, a native of the Wayne County village of Palmyra had a major role in securing this status for our country.

His name was William Thomas Sampson, and the naval victory at Santiago, Cuba in July, 1898, was afterwards clouded in sharp controversy, simply because Admiral Sampson was not present at the battle.

The house in which the future admiral was born on February 9, 1840, stands at Johnson and Vienna Streets in Palmyra, with a state historic marker implanted outside.

Of Scottish-Irish stock, the family was middle class. Will Sampson was quiet, industrious, solid and dependable, but not flashy. When 17, a friend declined appointment to the Naval Academy, Will went in his stead. He was graduated at the top of his class in 1861, in time to serve in the Civil War.

After sea duty, he was promoted to lieutenant, serving as an instructor at Annappolis before another tour at sea. On an ironclad, which was torpedoed in Charleston harbor in 1865, he escaped injury. Between wars, he served in many capacities. For

The man who planned the naval battle of Santiago, Cuba, Palmyra's native son, Admiral William T. Sampson.

four years he was superintendent of the Naval Academy. He was chief of naval ordinance, wrote textbooks, lectured at the Naval War College, and helped greatly in building a new navy of the most modern ships and equipment.

In 1894–95, the Venezuelan boundry dispute caused a war threat. President Grover Cleveland needed a new name to command the Atlantic battle fleet, and in reviewing the eligibles list, came to the record of William T. Sampson. "That is the man we want," said the President. The war scare faded through arbitration, but the situation in Cuba under Spain's oppressive rule was becoming intolerable.

Following the destruction of the battleship *Maine* in Havana harbor on February 15, 1898, with a loss of 258, President McKinley named Sampson head of the Board of Inquiry. The group failed to fix responsibility, but the nation was so inflamed by the jingoist Hearst and Pulitizer press that war was inevitable. President McKinley tried to avoid conflict, but the voices of intervention forced it on him.

First triumph for American arms was Commodore George Dewey's smashing victory over Admiral Motojo's fleet in Manila Bay, May 1, 1898. While Dewey had been enroute to Manila, a Spanish fleet of four cruisers and three destroyers under Admiral Cervera, left Cadiz, Spain and via the Cape Verde Islands, steamed westward. The fleet's destination was unknown, and there was considerable fear that it would bombard the unprotected cities of our Atlantic Coast.

Our Atlantic fleet under Rear Admiral Sampson, including the Flying Squadron of Commodore Winfield Scott Schley, was patrolling the coast of Cuba. But somehow, the Spaniards slipped into Santiago harbor unseen. Finally learning this, the Americans established a blockade off the port with the cruisers *New York* and *Brooklyn* and the battleships *Texas, Massachusetts, Iowa* and *Oregon.*

The last had just completed a spectacular 14,000 mile forced-draft run from the Bremerton Navy Yard near Seattle, via Cape Horn. Her officers and crew under Captain Clarke feared that they would arrive too late to be of any assistance to the Atlantic fleet. However, the voyage showed the vital necessity for an isthmian canal.

The blockade of Santiago was in force the entire month of June. In an effort to further impede egress from the port, Lt. Richmond Pearson Hobson, with a select group of volunteers, tried to block the channel by sinking an old collier, *Merrimac.* Under heavy fire from the nearby forts, which shot away the rudder, the ship sank, but didn't block the channel completely. The exploit of the handsome officer suddenly made him a hero, especially among the ladies. "Hobson's choice" was a phrase coined at this time.

As the month ended, the American Army of 16,000 outside Santiago was in a desperate situation. Disease attacked the men, food (especially beef) had spoiled, and reinforcements from the States were weeks away. General Shafter, ill with fever and gout, considered withdrawing his forces from the heights they so laboriously gained, and might be driven off from fire of Cervera's fleet in the harbor below. He requested Admiral Sampson to visit him to discuss the situation, and the cruiser *New York* was detached from the blockade for this purpose.

However, fate was to smile again on the Americans. Sunday morning, July 3, 1898, was hot and sunny. A lookout, spotting black smoke in the harbor, cried, "Here they come!" Battle flags broke out, guns were unlimbered, everyone sprung into action on the double. In single file, past the sunken *Merrimac,* the Spanish ships emerged from their anchorage and started to run westward along the shore. With Admiral Sampson eight miles away, Commodore Schley was the ranking officer.

Following their chief's previously formulated plans, the Americans weighed anchor and went after the Spaniards. The Yankee marksmanship was deadly. One by one the Spanish ships, wrecked and in flames, headed for the shore. The last one, the *Cristobal Colon,* named for the explorer who four centuries earlier had claimed for Spain the part of the western world now slipping from her grasp, was driven onto the beach by the relentless fire of the *Brooklyn* and *Oregon.*

The stunning four-hour battle proved the great superiority of the American naval establishment which Sampson (and the assistant secretary of the Navy, Theodore Roosevelt) had built into peak condition. "Shots which count" had been the byword of gunnery training for years. The Americans lost one killed (yeoman Ellis of the *Brooklyn*) and one wounded. Ten thousand dollars repaired the meager damage to the American ships. Five hundred Spaniards were killed, 1700 taken prisoner. The total would have been much larger if the Americans hadn't rescued many struggling in the water, including Admiral Cervera, who sent a warm letter of appreciation to Admiral Sampson.

When Samson sent his famous cablegram to President McKinley, announcing "A Fourth of July present to the nation: the Spanish fleet at Santiago," the American people were thrilled beyond measure. Coming on the heels of Dewey's victory at Manila Bay but two months previously, these events gave Americans a pride in their country, their Navy and their leaders, which they hadn't known since the Civil War.

But then came the controversy which was to take the shine off the accomplishment and furnish material for discussion for years. Schley had been in immediate command at the battle and was most affable and loquacious with the press. In most cases, the correspondents gave credit to the Commodore and neglected Admiral Sampson, who had laid out the plan of battle. Sampson, dignified and reserved, was not a politician given to blowing his own horn.

A long, bitter quarrel ensued between supporters of both men. Schley's previous record was attacked. All this delayed promotions of both. In 1901, a court of inquiry was held. While it did not praise Sampson, it criticized Schley for previous shortcomings. The majority of the court held that Schley merited censure. Admiral Dewey disagreed and presented a minority report which sustained Schley and gave him credit for the victory.

Weary from the in-fighting and bickering, Sampson visited Palmyra in the fall of 1899. There he had courted his first wife, Margaret Addison. To them were born five daughters, most of whom would marry naval officers. His second wife, Elizabeth Burling of Canandaigua, bore him two sons who served in the Navy in World War II.

On May 6, 1902, Admiral William T. Sampson died in Washington. A state funeral was held in the Capitol, burial with full honors in Arlington National Cemetery. The Buffalo Press chose the occasion for the following eulogy:

"There is no question among . . . experts as to who earned the credit for the victory at Santiago . . . The man who won the victory was the man whose tireless energy during 39 days and nights . . . had kept the fleet in such a state of preparation that victory was assured at any hour, day or night, of that long period when the Spaniards cared to take chances of battle; that no special orders were necessary when the critical moment came; that it was of no importance who the officer in actual command happened to be at the moment of battle. Admiral Sampson did this, and those who fancy it was a trifling task, have small knowledge of the history of naval warfare."

The natives of Palmyra, New York, we are sure, can justly be proud of their famous son, regardless of the dispute. In 1903, the Navy Department sent to the village a cannon, taken from the Spanish warship *Oquandro* of Santiago fame. It was dedicated and still stands in the village park, a fitting and lasting memorial to the Hero of Santiago, Admiral William Thomas Sampson.

When these first-grade pupils were photographed at Irondequoit's Hosea Rogers School in June 1930, School District 3 was operating on a $93,300 budget. The scowling youngster in the top row, extreme left, is the author.

LOW COST OF EDUCATION IN THE THIRTIES

July 1985

Is there anyone around who remembers when an Irondequoit school district could be operated for less than $100,000 a year? It was rather easy 56 years ago, considering that old District 3 had but one school, and teachers' salaries and benefits were a fraction of the inflated figures of today.

Not long ago, we came upon a pamphlet which was distributed to residents who attended a special meeting at the old red school at Titus Avenue and Cooper Road on July 18, 1927. The reason for the meeting was to vote on expansion of school facilities because of the growing population of District 3.

The voters at the meeting approved the following:

1. A four-room "portable" annex for the school, costing $12,000. Short-term notes were issued, spreading the cost over several years. The State Department of Education had refused to sanction construction of a permanent addition on the site.

2. Purchase of a 10–acre tract at the rear of the Sarah Howard and George Hallauer farms on Hudson Avenue for $32,000. Hosea Rogers grade school was built there.

3. Purchase of the 36–acre farm of H. J. Williams on the east side of Cooper Road for construction of a new grade school (Reuben A. Dake) and a new high school, for $75,000. Thirty-

year bonds retired interest and principal at $6,500 per year.

Before the special meeting, a citizens' advisory committee of 22 men was consulted by the school board. After studying all ramifications of the proposed expansion program, they unanimously recommended board and public approval. Committee members were: Rufus Anderson, W. G. Bevin, A. J. Bristol, Charles W. Curtis, C. W. Dean, Dr. Ralph L. Dublin, R. H. Farmen, Samual V. Gianniny, William Hamann, Louis Hawes, Walter C. Hess, W. A. Milligan, J. H. Muxworthy, John C. Oldenburg, O. L. Pritchard, H. M. Reinhard, C. C. Rogers, R. S. Rudman, E. W. Smallridge, George C. Tschume, William A. Yeager, and Oscar E. Zabel.

Perusing old newspapers one day, we came upon an item relative to District 3 (since merged with District 4 to form the W. Irondequoit School District). It is dated August 5, 1929, and should be of interest to those who "remember when." The names of teachers should be especially nostalgic. The story refers to the annual meeting of the board of education, slated to be held on August 6, 1929, in the auditorium of the "old school" at Titus and Cooper. That building would become Irondequoit High for hundreds of students in the years ahead.

Members of the board were Frank L. Grant, Roy V. Potteiger, Dwight C. DeWeese, Walter H. Mulcock and Ernest Petry. Terms of the first two were expiring, to be filled by election of their successors at the meeting. Special agenda considered where parents would be sending their grammar school children when Hosea Rogers School opened in September. Construcion of that school began in September, 1928.

"Built of light brick in modern collegiate style, it has two stories and a basement. Besides 16 classrooms, the school has a gymnasium, auditorium, library, health room and office." The school was erected for $195,000.

The board prepared a statement, sent to parents in the district, which said in part:

> There are more than 1000 persons in this district who are entitled to vote at these meetings, and when the importance of the matters voted upon, and the election of members of the school board in whom extensive powers are vested are considered, it seems unreasonable that with rare exceptions, fewer than 100 votes have been cast at these meetings.
>
> The board takes this opportunity to present the boundary limits which establish the attendance of pupils for the new school. Starting from the new building, the boundary runs north to a point on the north side of Titus Avenue, representing the east line of what or will be house No. 426, then west to the east side of Cedarwood Road, then north to the end of Cedarwood, then west including Pontiac Drive to the city line, following the line around the western and southern limits of District No. 3 to the east side of Portland Avenue, then north on Portland to a point representing what is or will be house No. 1880. From this point, the boundary line runs westward to the new school, including all of Stanton Road and Hudson Avenue as far north as what is or will be house No. 1880.
>
> The board asks cooperation in this boundary plan until after the school registration is completed, after which adjustments will be considered by the principals. These boundaries apply only to the pupils in grades up to and including the sixth grade. All pupils of the junior and senior high school will attend the old school, regardless of where they live in the district.

In addition to adopting the boundaries at the annual meeting, the board approved the annual budget for 1929–30, amounting to $93,300. This represented an increase of $5,800 above the previous year, due to increased teacher requirements and anticipated operation of the new school.

Salaries of the faculty for the school year totaled $59,175, distributed as follows: Charles W. Spangle, high school principal, $3,400; Mrs. Carolyn T. Simmons, Mrs. Florence A. Ladd and Royal W. Brown, $2,300 each; Mrs. Elizabeth Dufloo and Miss

Kathryn M. Shreder, $2,200 each; Carl L. Eklind, $2,100; Miss Harriet Middleton, $2,050; Mrs. Eva R. Sherman, $1,975; Miss Anna McCullock and Miss Julia B. Zuck, $1,900 each; Miss Helen L. Regensburger and Howard R. Johnson, $1,800 each; Miss J. Gertrude Dowling, $1,700; Miss Bernice Franke, $1,500; Tom Grierson, $1,000; and Mildred J. Merz, $900.

Hosea Rogers School Staff: Maude I. West, principal, $3,100; Anna T. Wynn, $1,975; Ernestine Blake, $1,950; Cecile R. Wright, $1,850; Emma E. Parsons, $1,750; Cecelia McCutcheon, $1,700; May A. Armstrong and Gladys M. Tuck, $1,675 each; M. Ellen Thompson and Ora M. Combs, $1,625 each; Charlotte J. Lamont, $1,600; Starr A. Basseti, $1,575; Blinetta Purtell and Frieda Iseman, $1,275 each; Helen L. Szathowski, $1,200. To use a time-worn cliche, times have certainly changed!

Another clipping, dated May, 1931, shows that Alfred C. Hamilton had arrived to examine Irondequoit High School and confer with the board of education. That September he succeeded Charles W. Spangle, who was retiring. Ultimately Hamilton was to become superintendent of District 3, in addition to his high school duties.

At the same time in 1931, it was announced that a new grade school would be built if the taxpayers approved. This building became Reuben A. Dake School on the multi-acre tract on Cooper Road. It was also stated that "in the next 15 years, it is hoped that a new high school would be built." What was to become the new Irondequoit High was realized about 23 years later, after World War II and merger of Districts 3 and 4.

Yes, it was easy to operate a school district for a modest sum in 1929. Since that time, a steadily rising birth rate, expanding housing development, a teachers' union, and the ravages of inflation conspired to make $100,000–a-year budgets and a $10–per-$1,000 tax rate but wistful memories to taxpayers.

ROCHESTER TO MOUNT MORRIS ON THE ERIE

March 1986

Of the six interurban electric lines which radiated from Rochester, the one which didn't achieve the popularity of others, yet carried a fair share of passengers during its heyday, was the branch of the Erie Railroad to Mount Morris. During its existence, it utilized three kinds of motive power.

The line had its beginnings on June 7, 1851, when the Rochester and Genesee Valley Railroad was organized, with the provision that it "could continue for 200 years." James S. Wadsworth and Freeman Clarke were prime movers. Basic reasons for the new company were to create passenger transportation facilities and to connect with the Pennsylvania coal mines. Work on the road began in 1853.

The first 18.4 miles, which began at the rear of the county jail on Rochester's Exchange Street, ended at the sulphur springs in Avon, where it connected with the Erie, which was building lines west to Buffalo and south to its main line at Corning. In 1856, capital stock of $300,000 was issued for the organization of a second entity, the Genesee Valley Railroad Company, for building a line from Avon to Mount Morris, a distance of about 16 miles.

On January 1, 1859, the first steam train entered Geneseo,

and in April, Mount Morris. Total cost was over $295,000. In 1873, the road was leased to the Erie Railroad, Jay Gould as trustee. For the remainder of its life, the Erie was the parent company.

For 48 years, the motive power on the Rochester-Mount Morris division was steam. In 1904, the Erie engaged Westinghouse, Church, Keir & Co., to provide estimates on electrifying the line, and the Avon-Corning division. The latter estimate was deemed too costly, and that section was never converted.

Work began on electrifying the Mount Morris division on June 6, 1906. Catenary overhead was installed to support the power lines carrying 25–cycle current at 11,000 volts, single-phase, the first of its kind in the country. An electric switching station was built at Mortimer, and a transformer plant at Golah sent power to the Avon substation. From Rochester to Avon, the transmission line was located on Erie property for most of the distance. The wire support system consisted of 40–foot cypress poles, joined above the tracks in an A-frame. Lighting protectors were installed on every fifth pole, and the distance between poles was 220 feet, shorter on curves. Telegraph and telephone cables were buried beneath the track at crossings. Track, originally laid with 68–lb. rail, was renewed with 80–lb. rail.

The line utilized a number of bridges, the largest being one over the Genesee River, 1.5 miles south of Rochester. There were truss bridges at Rush and over Canaseraga Creek. A most beautiful one was the five-arch stone bridge over Conesus Creek at Ashantee. Still standing, it is a potent monument to its designers and builders.

While work on the electrification was progressing, the Erie ordered six passenger cars from the St. Louis Car Co. They weighed 48 tons, were 51 feet long overall. Also ordered were

Scenes along the Rochester-Mount Morris division of the Erie.

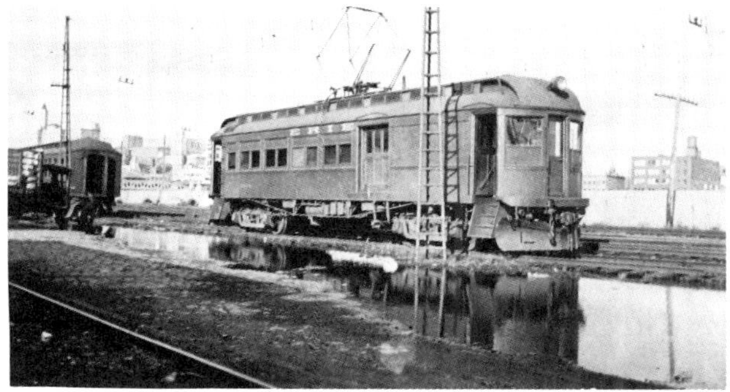

3104 at Rochester junction.

Typical passenger car.

Four-car trains were common in the days of excursions to the Conesus Lake area.

one combination baggage-passenger car and four passenger-smoker trailers. According to employees, the cars provided excellent service and always were able to buck deep snowdrifts. Some were equipped with small V-plows in lieu of a pilot. Even in spring when the Genesee overflowed at Mortimer and Golah, the cars could get through. Scheduled speed was 29 mph, and they were equipped for multiple-unit operation. Of interest was the unique method of current collection employed by cars of the division. They used European-style pantographs. No other line upstate and very few interurban railways in the country had them.

The electrification work was pushed as rapidly as the weather allowed. Seven and a half months after its start, the first official trip was made between Rochester and Avon. The 18 miles were covered in 39 minutes. It was hoped that completion of the work would enable cars to run in regular service by March, 1907. However, severe winter storms held up construcion and it wasn't until May 11, 1907, that a special train with newspapermen made the trip to Mount Morris. The travelers dined at the Scoville House, visited the Avon shops, and returned to Rochester.

The following day, regular service began, 13 trains a day leaving Rochester. A three-inch snowfall caused problems when insulators became balky. Steam power took over for three days as insulators were replaced and some servicing was done on car motors. Throughout its history, the electric cars shared the rails with steam trains on the Mount Morris run, as freight was carried as well.

How many remember the stops along the way? There were South Park, Westfall, Crittenden, Mortimer, Bailey's, Fenners, Brooks, W. Henrietta, Martin, Blair, Industry, Gannett, Golah, Meadow-Wood, Elm Place, Wiards, Avon, Ashante, Fowler, S. Avon, Houston, Seven Nations, Geneseo, Cuylerville, Jones,

Shakers, and Mount Morris. At the last stop, connections could be made with the Dansville & Mount Morris Railroad, and at Avon one could board a train on the Livonia, Avon & Lakeville Railroad for Conesus and the lake steamers.

Rochester had two Erie stations. The first was on the site of what was later Swift and Co. property on Exchange Street, south of the area of the troup-Howell Bridge. It was a one-story structure and opened in 1897. Of Philadelphia pressed brick, having a carved veranda surrounding it, and a waiting room done in Corinthian style, it was something to see. The train room was 270 feet long and 65 feet wide. Total cost was $600,000.

The second station was situated on Court Street, between the Genesee River and the Carroll-Fitzhugh raceway, on the site once occupied by Delano's Planing Mills. The passenger depot, built of red brick and facing Court Street, was two stories high, surmounted by a clock tower. The top floor was for offices, ground floor for waiting rooms and ticket offices. The train shed was at the south end. On the west side were storage tracks, capable of holding 25 passenger cars. Interurbans from several lines had their layovers here before the Rochester Subway was built. On the river side, there was sufficient area for hotel carryalls, private carriages and autos. Fronting on Exchange Street was the freight house, 400 feet long, 60 feet wide and two stories high.

The Mount Morris division once handled a high of 24 trains a day. Especially on Sundays during the summer picnic and boating season, traffic was heavy. After World War I, with the rise of the automobile, traffic took a nose dive on the electric line. By 1931 only 12 trains a day were run. On November 29, 1934, the juice was turned off for the last time and only one gas-electric car provided passenger service until September 30, 1941, when that ended, and trackage was torn up from Avon to Mount Morris.

Bit by bit the last vestiges of the once-proud Mount Morris division of the Erie became memories. The Rochester station's famous clock tower to which thousands directed their gaze in checking their watches, was removed in 1939. In 1941, the train shed was razed and six years later, the remainder of the station was but a memory. The freight house continued operations for about 30 years. It was cut into in the early 1950s to allow for the construction of the approach to the Troup-Howell Bridge on the west end.

Thus, with successive passing of the electric cars, the station and its clock tower, and all passenger service, the curtain was lowered on the last interurban line to operate from Rochester. It was a great era, and those fortunate enough to have lived during its existence have memories of a delightful segment of the American past which contributed to the growth and prosperity of our country.

CHARLOTTE'S BLAST FURNACE

June 1986

Rochester is known as a city of light industry, specializing in the highly technical field. However, there was a period in which a heavy industry flourished. This centered on the blast furnace in the village of Charlotte.

The facility was located on 16 acres in the area bounded by Lake Avenue, Beach Avenue and 1200 feet along the Genesee River. The property, involving Lot Parcels 23, 24, 25, and 26 was purchased for $9500 from the Pulteney and Benjamin F. Barney heirs. To John M. French belongs the credit for conceiving the idea of iron manufacturing and locating it in the harbor area.

The Rochester Iron Manufacturing Co. built the furnace in 1868, and it was ready for use in January 1869, the year Charlotte was incorporated as a village. Total cost was $250,000. Officers of the firm were James Brackett, president; Burrell Spencer, vice president; George H. Dana, secretary and treasurer; Ezra Jones, D. D. Rand, Martin Briggs, Jarvis Lord, Charles H. Chapin, B. M. Baker and John Horton, trustees. Horton was also superintendent with Joseph T. Cox as his assistant.

The casting and furnace stack houses measured 104 feet by 127 feet. The stack was 22 feet in diameter and nearly 70 feet tall. The hoist for lifting ore was 60 feet high. The red brick in the buildings was made by Jones & Denise of Charlotte, contractor for the mason work was E. J. Green of Rochester, and the carpentry was by John W. Allen of Charlotte.

Toward the end of 1868, the first shipment of iron ore was delivered to the site, and in January, 1869, that load was poured into "pigs" as hundreds of onlookers marveled at the process. In a 24-hour period the furnace consumed about 100 tons of limestone and ore and 20 to 25 tons of coal, which produced 35 to 40 tons of pig iron. A staff of 25 to 30 men was initially employed.

During the first six months the facility produced more than 2500 tons of pig iron, which resulted in a five-per-cent dividend to shareholders. The new industry was welcomed, because it was believed it would enhance the importance of nearby Rochester. By the end of the first year of operation, the work force was upped to 90 men who produced 10,200 tons of pig iron.

For a few years, Arthur G. Yates ran the coal trestle and station, which occupied a portion of the waterfront east of the furnace. He had 31 coal bunkers, each with a capacity of 100 tons. During the first few months, he shipped in 30,000 tons of coal. The ore came by train from mines in Ontatio, New York and by ship from the Lake Superior region. This combination produced a superior foundry iron, combining strength with fluidity and especially adapted for stove plate and heavy or light castings.

Tracks of the Rome, Watertown & Ogdensburg Railroad (later the New York Central) passed the premises. Special sidings to service the facility were built, and a 900-foot dock nearby accomodated the ore carriers.

By 1879, the company was in financial difficulties and was purchased by Henry C. Roberts of Rochester with an offering of $125,000 and changed the firm's name to the Charlotte Iron Works. The next year $70,000 was spent for additions and improvements, including 12 steam boilers, each 65 feet long. Three 400-horsepower engines were in operation, driving wheels

24 feet in diameter and weighing 34 tons each. Seven thousand cubic feet of air per minute was forced into the stack and from there to the blast ovens, where the heat varied between 900 and 1000 degrees.

Fourteen thousand gallons of water were used per hour in the boilers. It was pumped from the river through a 600-foot intake by a Worthington compound pump. When the renovations were completed, it was claimed to be one of the best equipped furnaces in the country. In 1884, it produced 20,000 tons of pig iron.

A very pleasant way to spend the evening when one hosted out-of-town visitors was to take them to the furnace at the time of the casting process. Rivers of fire ran onto sand beds. When the last bed was reached, workmen in heavy-soled shoes

The Charlotte Blast Furnace. Seen are the tracks of the New York Central on which ore, coal and limestone were brought to the site. Now a graveled parking lot, the area lies adjacent to the Port of Rochester Terminal at Lake and Beach Avenues.

walked over the first beds, throwing sand over the cooling iron. A trip through the furnace's engine room, with its monstrous wheels which revolved in and out of a deep pit, was awe-inspiring. Also impressive were the great open caldrons, where the ore was dumped into a fiery mass of coal to convert it into a liquid, and the ovens, the open doors of which revealed scenes which made one recall Dante's *Inferno.*

Although Roberts ran the company, his other interests took him out of town frequently, and his wife, Julia, oversaw the operations at Charlotte. In addition to being an excellent businesswoman, she also was an accomplished telegrapher, and this talent was responsible for saving the furnace one cold winter night in 1884. Roberts was in Pennsylvania, and his wife received a phone call from the furnace office. (It was one of the first office-to-home phones in the area.) Mrs. Roberts learned that the coal supply was almost exhausted. Not enough remained to complete the smelting of ore then in the furnace. If the furnace cooled, the ore would be spoiled by solidifying, and the furnace also ruined. The necessary coal was in a nearby train, but deep snow prevented its delivery.

Mrs. Roberts called her brother, who commandeered a force of 25 snow shovelers. She then telegraphed the Utica office of the railroad and received an order for the train crew to follow as fast as the tracks were cleared. Just before dawn the siren was heard, the furnaces were clear and ready for a new supply of ore. Everything was under control. Exhausted, Mrs. Roberts "sat down and had a good cry."

After her husband's death the following year, the widow carried on as owner. In 1891, the plant was enlarged to manufacture iron pipe. The village of Charlotte was urged to remit local taxes for 10 years and to subscribe to $25,000 in stock.

Charlotte had but one labor strike in its history, that at the iron works in May, 1893. Owing to a change of superintendents and wages, dissension arose among the minority. Village president P. M. Schwartz took precautions to avoid trouble and detailed 12 additional police to the area. A deputy sheriff served papers on the ex-superintendent ending the strike, but none of the malcontents was retained.

In 1903, Mrs. Roberts sold the firm to McKinley & Corrigan Co. of Cleveland, which made necessary improvements to update the facility. In 1916, the year Charlotte was annexed to Rochester, the works closed for a few months. However, when World War I demanded more iron, the furnace roared night and day. The continuous chug-a-lug, chug-a-lug of the furnace and the celestial display, which could be seen for miles at night as it changed casts every four hours, was to become a poignant memory for Charlotters.

People ate, slept, played and worked to the sonorous thumpings and wheezings of this industrial giant. In 1916, 175 men were employed and 325 tons of iron were produced every 24 hours. Soon after the war, with the works' output limited, there were two long periods of idleness before the McKinley Co. reopened the facility in August, 1926. G. O. Hollenbough was sent from Cleveland to be superintendent of the 60 men who got the plant into working order. There were 60,000 tons of ore on the site and another 60,000 in Buffalo.

However, the plant operated only a few months until the ore was used up. Then it closed for good. The Cleveland firm sold the property to William Bausch for $800,000. He later sold it to the city for $225,000 after considerable controversy.

With the plant's razing imminent, Julia Roberts was interviewed at her home at 4752 Lake Avenue. "It is hard work, running a blast furnace, but there is a lot about it which is fascinating. In the days when my husband and I ran it, the men worked in 12-hour shifts. Now they work eight hours a day. But there are, even today, few easy jobs around a furnace."

Legends grew about the place. Children were told ghastly, hair-raising tales and were threatened with confinement in the place for misdeeds. A number of fatal accidents occurred there, and some were alleged to be the result of workers' plots. The most gruesome incident centered around the Cammorra Society. One of the workers was supposed to have revealed its secrets, and his fellow workers were delegated to wreak their vengeance.

As he was guiding a load of ore to the maw of one of the furnaces, something slipped, and car, ore and operator sped down the trestle into the furnace. No trace of the man was ever found. His friends simply knew that he had mysteriously disappeared at work, and no one connected the disappearance with an accident in which an ore car had fallen into the furnace. Safety measures were adopted, and after that no more workmen disappeared. Maybe they prudently didn't reveal secrets after what happened to their colleague!

In February 1927, razing of the facility was begun, and though it had benefitted Charlotte merchants for more than 55 years, regrets at its passing were few. The S. Snyder Corporation and the William H. Wilson Iron Works Company demolished the structures. Tons of steel and iron scrap went to out-of-town smelters. C. P. Ward, Inc., purchased nine carloads of railroad rails, which were cut into suitable lengths for manhole roofs.

The Newport Sand & Gravel Co. and the Builders Supply Co. each purchased a giant hopper, 31 feet by 31 feet. The transport of these devices across Stutson Street Bridge and up St. Paul Boulevard required the service of a wire wagon from the New York State Railways to keep trolley wires and supports clear. No dynamite was used in razing the plant. The last building to be demolished was a three-story brick powerhouse.

Thus, an ususual era in the industrial life of the community passed into history. There are still some residents of the area who remember the chug-a-lug of the engines and the pyrotechnic display in the skies over Charlotte when the furnace was fired—sounds and sights which are but memories, never to return.

Typeset on an Itek Digitek 3000 photocompositor in 11/15 Garamond with Helvetica light used for captions.

Printed on 60 pound book white and perfect bound with a 10 point coated one-side-cover.

Contact Walt Steesy for your book publishing needs.

A *Quality* publication from
Heart of the Lakes Publishing
Interlaken, New York 14847